NAVIGATING THROUGH CHANGE

Harry Woodward, Ph.D.

with Mary Beckman Woodward

Boston, Massachusetts   Burr Ridge, Illinois
Dubuque, Iowa   Madison, Wisconsin   New York, New York
San Francisco, California   St. Louis, Missouri

For Elizabeth and Nathaniel

on the eve of their entry
to a white-water world

McGraw-Hill

A Division of The McGraw·Hill Companies

Library of Congress Cataloging-in-Publication Data

Woodward, Harry.
  Navigating through change / by Harry Woodward with Mary Beckman Woodward.
     p.   cm.
   Includes index.
   ISBN 0-7863-0233-X
   1. Organizational change.   I. Woodward, Mary Beckman.   II. Title.
HD58.8.W673   1994
658.4'06—dc20
                                                                93–48345

Printed in the United States of America

6 7 8 9 0   BKM BKM   9 0 9

Acknowledgments

This book owes many things to many people—most particularly to the people and organizations with whom I have worked over the past 10 years. Special thanks go to Henry Griffiths of IBM—UK for his collaboration and support early on in the process; to Lynn Swensen and Robert Blomberg for enabling me to work in the healthcare industry, and to Robert for providing ongoing insights and opportunities in that field; to Ed Griffin for keeping me connected with the changes in academia; and to Yoshi Ueno of Learning Masters International in Tokyo for the opportunity to work and learn in Japan.

Thanks also go to Lanny Schmidt for helping me find my way through the intricacies of chaos theory; to John Iacovini for his support and insights in the area of human motivation; and with high regard to Ed Garcia for his friendship, his contributions in the area of self management and for his careful reading and valuable comments on the book's initial manuscript.

I also want to gratefully acknowledge the support of Dr. Walter Daves of Georgia State University and John Corbett and Rebecca Stephens of International Learning Inc. for their development and validation of my rough ideas into what is now the *Change Readiness Survey*.

To my colleagues at Stackhouse Garber and Associates I extend both a thank-you for your ongoing support and ideas and a heartfelt wish for a prosperous future.

I would be remiss if I didn't also pay a special thank-you to Bonny Luthy of ProtoType Services for her professionalism and creativity in the preparation of the many versions of the manuscript, as well as all the other related materials I am constantly throwing at her—usually on tight time frames.

I want to particularly acknowledge the people who, over the years, whether they were aware of it or not, taught me valuable lessons about change; they include Norm Anderson, Dan Brunet,

William Bridges, Steve Buchholz, Luis Collazo, Daryl Conner, Gerald Dahl, Tom DuFresne, Jon Enright, Page Glasgow, Karen Johnson, Mat Juechter, Rob Koch, George Land, Hal McLean, Pat O'Malley, Tom Roth, Jane Stubblefield, Mark Tager, Allan Talley, Karon Wendt, Larry Wilson, and Mike Zosel.

I owe a special expression of gratitude, in memorium, for John Williamson, the measure of whose loss is exceeded only by the depth of his friendship and wisdom.

Finally, for her support and insight as well as her valuable contributions to both the spirit and substance of the book, I want to thank my life partner in change, my wife Mary—whose idea it was in the first place.

Preface

N one other than management expert Peter Drucker has stated unequivocally that "every organization of today has to build into its very structure *the management of change*."[1] Drucker is not alone. The current demand to meet the challenge of change is not a theme but an anthem. Calls to "thrive on chaos" and to "create your future" echo from every corner of the business and organizational world. Unfortunately, this heady rhetoric often bypasses the core needs of those on whom the success of the change ultimately depends—the people who have to *manage* it.

In a recent series of interviews, managers who were either in the midst of or had just come through an initial wave of major change were asked to comment on their experiences. They said:

> They told me the change would be like the flicker of a lightbulb. They were wrong. It was a total blackout. My regular skills didn't work for me anymore and I ended up feeling my way in the dark.

> The one thing that I know *I* didn't anticipate was the severity of the impact on the staff.

> I tried to assure people, but something—maybe it was my own misgivings—seemed to keep creeping through. The more I talked, the less they believed me—or trusted me.

> They told me to "get creative and come up with some new approaches." But the real message was: Don't screw it up! They wanted trial and error—without the error.

> It's still without a doubt the worst experience of my career as a manager.

These are candid comments from managers on the front lines; from the people who have to make the change work. Far from being exhilarated, their experience of change is one of pain. Managers in this position are often intellectually in tune with, but operationally remote from, the rhetoric of becoming "change agents" and "reinventing the future." As one manager put it, "I don't mind change. It's *changing* that concerns me."

Managers in today's changing environment too often are condemned to try to solve new problems with old tools or are supplied with new approaches and innovations which do not meet the demands of their day-to-day jobs. This dilemma applies particularly to the intensified *human* aspects of that job. Indeed, the human response—more specifically, the "people breakage" that accompanies change—tends to be neglected, whether the organization is in acceptance or denial. Whether attempting to go back to basics or pushing out the envelope, organizations in the throes of change tend to fixate on their systems and procedures. They create a situation, as one person put it, "like that of a top-notch hospital emergency room team, so intent on preparing and fine-tuning their equipment that they forget about the patient lying in a corner, slowly bleeding to death."

Purpose

The purpose of *Navigating through Change* is to provide a means for understanding change and, more importantly, a set of key skills for managing: managing yourself, managing your operation, and managing your people—in an environment of continual change. Although personal and organizational change are very complex phenomena, there are models which can simplify, without oversimplifying. There are constructs which will enable people to orient themselves and create a context for action. The skills presented are not recipes, but rather templates that can be immediately adapted and used in your organization.

The skills and approaches presented here are what we have discovered are the core competencies for managing and surviving in a changing environment. More than just the basics or "first aid," these skills and approaches are the cornerstones for creating a successful change culture. They function to meet the initial and then the ongoing needs of people and organizations in continual chaos. As such, these skills open doors. The strategies presented here meet the immediate need and create a receptive host for subsequent approaches to the same issues.

My tenure in the area of change spans 20 years of working with a wide variety of Fortune 500 organizations, as well as a number of smaller organizations, in the financial, high-tech, automotive, manufacturing, telecommunications, retail, and transportation industries. Also reflected in this book are my experiences with government, health care, colleges, and universities, and a number of international organizations.

In all, *Navigating through Change* takes its primary cue from the word *navigating*. As one change expert observes, "The whole idea that a map can be drawn in advance of an innovative journey through turbulent times is a fantasy."[2] He's right. The map cannot be prepared in advance; nor, indeed, can the final destination be plotted with any degree of certainty. But the tools and provisions for the journey are a different matter—particularly if we can base our selection of these tools on the experiences of people who have made similar trips. I hope the skills and strategies recommended in this book will be useful to you in your experience of change.

Contents

Chapter One, on "taking chaos seriously," defines the context of the current situation by identifying the key forces shaping change in organizations. This chapter also clarifies the nature of the current change environment—how it differs from "normal" change and what kinds of new tools we need to address it. In this chapter we will draw on some of the discoveries in the emerging field of chaos theory to help us understand the nature of continually changing, that is "chaotic," environments. And we will suggest some principles for operating in such an environment.

Chapter Two, on "skills for a new context," begins by looking at the experiences of people caught up in change and, more specifically, the job of the manager in a change process. This chapter outlines a general change strategy for managers and leaders and concludes by identifying and explaining the four key skills for successful change management. These skills will provide the basis for a practical approach to establishing a change culture in an organization.

Chapter Three, on "developing openness," examines the differences between "real goals" and "stated goals," that is, the difference between what I *say* I want and what I *really* want. Making this distinction is the beginning of the first task in the change process: managing yourself and developing personal "openness." Too many managers enter into the change process as a "house divided," saying one thing and feeling another. This chapter will allow you to look at your own stated and real goals and decide if they are opposed to each other or in sync with each other. Only when you come to terms with your own reactions and intentions can you act coherently and foster a sense of trust in others.

Chapter Four, on "communicating change," examines how the current practices or "norms" for communication in many organizations do not fully meet the operational or human needs of people in change. A constantly changing environment requires that you communicate more often and less formally—often with information that may seem sketchy or liable to be quickly outdated. As a result, many managers avoid or procrastinate telling people what is going on for fear that they will appear unprepared or not in control. How you handle information and, more importantly, how you handle yourself when you communicate is a key factor in your credibility and effectiveness. This chapter then offers some specific methods and techniques to set up an ongoing and effective communication system designed for organizations in change.

Chapter Five, on "supporting people in transition," examines the basic reactions of people when they are faced with changes. It examines both the negative and positive aspects of these reactions. Managing change is, to a large degree, managing people through a difficult transition. It requires skill and sensitivity. Indeed, the job of a manager in this process is not so much that of a problem solver as it is that of a "movement starter"—someone responsible for helping people begin to move through the change process. The chapter offers insights and strategies for supporting people, a skill which one researcher has established as the single, most effective skill needed by managers of change.

Chapter Six, on "creating a learning organization," addresses the issues of "learning how to learn" in a chaotic environment. We begin with an examination of the roles of intuition, of personal knowledge, and even of humor, and how they help us discern key issues and generate ideas. Later, we will suggest specific techniques for generating and implementing ideas—techniques that establish learning as a tool for change.

Chapter Seven, "navigating through change," offers insights and skills in two specific change-implementation areas:

1. Working backward, moving forward—a method for setting and revising goals in an environment that is continually changing. Setting a direction in a chaotic, fluid environment relies less on up-front planning than on midcourse observation and correction. This section provides examples and skills for change navigation.

2. Positive contention—given the need to constantly generate new ideas, a change environment must be willing to accept not only discussion but even argument and disagreement. Indeed, one of the key strategies in successful change management is to set up self-organizing networks that actually encourage open conflict and dialogue around problems and ideas. This section describes skills for contending positively to make decisions and implement ideas.

Taken as a whole, *Navigating through Change* provides practical means for grounding yourself in the change process and developing a core set of skills for establishing and sustaining a change culture.

Harry Woodward
Mary Beckman Woodward

Contents

Racing Shells and Rubber Rafts

The crew arrives early in the morning. The captain unlocks the padlock on the rough wood door. The door swings open allowing the morning light to fall on the hull of the racing shell. The crew members, some of them still yawning, walk the boat down to the dock at the river's edge, flip it upright and set it gently in the water. Within minutes the racing shell cuts through the glassy surface of the water in gentle, silent surges. On the shore, a passerby hears a faint dip, dip, dip as the boat glides through the morning mist coming off the water.

A racing shell on the water is a classic image of beauty: the burnished wood hull, long and sleek; the brass fittings; the precise movements of the crew in their school-color jerseys; the rhythmic cadence of the coxswain. The racing shell's crew is also a classic image of cooperation. Along with football teams and symphony orchestras, racing crews are one of the most often depicted and overused example of people working in harmony toward a common goal. Theirs is an ideal world in which every individual knows his or her job and relies on the benevolent direction of the leader and the cooperation of all the parts to achieve efficiency, harmony, and success.

But what happens if we put this boat—and its crew—into the Colorado River?

The images of beauty and efficiency quickly dissolve. The craft is tragically ill-suited to the foaming mountains of white water. The notion of a coxswain calling cadences or crew members trying to pull in unison becomes farcical. The craft takes on water. Its pointed bow lunges out of the water and shatters on a rock. Putting the shell and its crew in the river was a mistake, the same mistake that characterizes many people and organizations today: assuming that stable systems can function successfully in an unstable environment.

What kind of boat is better suited to white water? Obviously, a rubber raft. Not as sleek, not as efficient, and certainly not as orderly as the racing shell, the rubber raft is nevertheless the ideal craft for the river. It is flexible and resilient. It can arch and bend to the constantly changing contours of the river. It can sustain bumps and can pivot and find its direction again. It can take on water and remain afloat. Its crew members are trained in a variety of skills from paddling . . . to pushing off . . . to steering.

They vary their skills on a moment-by-moment basis. Their leader is not above bailing, nor is any crew member barred from navigating. In all, the yellow rubber raft—although not as pretty or romantic as the pristine racing shell—is a much healthier image for the organizational and interpersonal needs of people in change.

However, to what extent do people in organizations truly accept the fact that the change they are experiencing requires something unique from them? To what extent are terms such as "permanent white-water" and "rubber rafts" more than just rhetoric and jargon? Finally, to what extent is change really changing, and if it is, what can we do about it?

Chapter One

Charting the Flow: Taking Chaos Seriously

To reject one paradigm without simultaneously substituting another is to reject science itself.

> Thomas S. Kuhn
> *The Structure of Scientific Revolutions*

Where chaos begins, classical science stops

> James Gleick
> *Chaos: Making a New Science*

We need to think more deeply about the nature of instability and why we equate it with failure.

> Ralph D. Stacey
> *Managing the Unknowable*

Do we have a problem or don't we?

W hen executives, managers, and workers involved in change ask themselves "do we have problem?" they usually refer to duration. The *know* they have a problem. What they are really asking is: Will it go away by itself? Is it in our power to make it go away? Or is it here to stay? They hope for the former but dread or deny the latter.

I recently worked with a large and rapidly growing Fortune 500 high-tech firm. Theirs was an organization in which rapid change was a given, and high tolerance to ambiguity a job requirement. They were the classic old hands at change. Their latest strategic decision, however, was a major change even by their standards. As a result, they were beginning to see disruption and mild forms of dysfunctional behavior. Some recognized this behavior, others did not.

One general manager, who had been with the company from the beginning, was obviously upset by the change in the culture. The new plan called for a more controlled disbursement of internal resources and for the first time he was seeing hoarding, withholding of information, and unhealthy internal competition. He was upset by the sudden loss of camaraderie and teamwork he had sought to build over the years.

When I asked him what he was going to do about it, he answered absently, "Well, I guess I'll have to do *something* won't I." The more he talked, the more he reminded himself what was happening, and the more he reminded himself, the more he wanted to forget it. He ended our discussion somewhat abruptly, remarking in the spirit of Scarlet O'Hara, that he would think about it tomorrow. He had meetings to attend today.

Elsewhere in upper management, the chairman was acutely aware of the reaction and the potential for dysfunction. However, the president denied it. When I asked him if he thought this change was any different than changes in the past, he answered flatly, "Nope." That was the end of it as far as he was concerned.

PICTURES THAT CONVINCE

This organization's discussion of "do we have a problem, or don't we?" was resolved in an interesting way. After the issue was debated to abstraction, something concrete came into the scene. In sessions with employees, one of the exercises asked participants to draw a picture of the company. The results were quite compelling and so were presented at the executive committee meeting. The company's upper management was struck by pictures of a plane flying upside-down on fire, of a traffic clover leaf with no exits, and of an employee trapped in an hourglass trying to avoid being squeezed through the middle. These pictures were powerful incarnations of existing organizational and people issues clearly showing that something had changed; and on the basis of these impassioned drawings, upper management reluctantly agreed that change was indeed an issue. "If people are drawing the company like that, then we'd better pay attention," one officer said.

After almost a decade of working to understand organizational and personal change, I have found that the simple pictures people use to represent their organizations are powerful indicators of what is taking place. The images started out for the most part as what I like to call "life images." Although beleaguered and often assailed on all sides, the organization was depicted as a tree, a ship under full sail, healthy people flexing their muscles, or buildings brimming with positive activity and energy. Granted, there were missing limbs and threatening bugs on the trees, icebergs and marauding sharks in the water, Band-Aids and overloaded dumbbells on the people, and cracks in the buildings. But in general, change was represented as external irritants which, the images implied, could be staved off through fast action and recommitment to the organization and its goals.

As time went on and the 80s gave way to the 90s, these images began to change. The trees began to die, the ships began to sink, the people began to lose weight and get trapped, and the buildings began to crumble. The presentations of these pictures by the small groups assigned to draw them became more sarcastic and pointed. In one picture of a sinking ship the company flag flew high on the mast, but the employees, chained to their oars, had slipped below the waterline. The ship's wheelhouse was abandoned because the captain and crew had escaped in balloons.

Images of things turned upside down, people encased in glass, dead ends, things on fire, abandonment, and blindfolded people trying to pin the tail on nonexistent donkeys began to abound. Gambling themes—pinball machines, crap shoots, ring tosses, and horse races—started to increase. Many depicted people falling. One group cut out a lot of little stick people, cradled them in the paper, and when they held up the image of their company, they shook the paper and all the little stick people slid off and fell to the floor. The other participants howled with laughter, but it was a laugh of recognition, not amusement.

Do these people have bad attitudes? Are they just being overly perverse and negative? Or is this just a little cathartic good fun? I think not. These images come from the heart. These people feel release when they discover they are not alone in their pain and have a chance to express their true feelings and be heard. The energy is still there, as is the willingness to work hard and be committed. What is missing is a sense of direction and knowledge of how to apply that energy—or even where to go.

It is dangerous to play armchair psychologist, but when I look at these pictures and talk to the people who draw them, certain things seem very clear. Like children's drawings, what these images may lack in artistic talent, they more than make up for in honesty. What they are saying can be summed up in three words: *aimlessness*, *abandonment*, and *ignorance*.

People in a constantly changing environment feel aimless. They feel like they have energy, but no direction nor any context to understand what is happening to them. They are engaged in energetic, but ultimately unfocused, even erratic, behavior. Thus they draw themselves rowing furiously, driving around and around on traffic loops, shooting dice, and trying to benchpress impossible weights.

People in change often feel abandoned. They feel that others— the organization ("they")—don't care; and that "they" are too busy, either laying their plans or plotting their escapes, to care about the problems of the people in the trenches. Thus they depict themselves as falling, sinking, shrinking, and freezing.

People in the midst of change feel ignorant. They want to learn so that they can survive. They want know what needs to be accomplished and what skills it will take. They also want to teach. They want to share ideas they have, but they feel that nobody will listen. Thus they draw themselves as blind or blindfolded, chasing an elusive donkey; encased in glass, mouthing words no one can hear; or sitting in a sea of parts with no directions on how to assemble them.

Lest I paint too grim a picture, I should also mention that the drawings of people in the throes of change still contain a healthy measure of human life images as well as images of new trees sprouting up, survivors in lifeboats making a new landfall, Arnold Schwarzenegger figures kicking in doors, and phoenixes rising from ashes.

These pictures give us a starting point. If aimlessness, abandonment, and ignorance are the symptoms, then direction, support, and learning may be the cures. It's time to start. We begin with direction. More specifically, we begin by creating a context, a means to understand the whole.

TOWARD A NEW CONTEXT

A river, as one geologist put it, "starts off in a groove and ends up in a rut." The same may be said for ideas, for science, for business. Certainly the same can be said for people and organizations in change. "Nothing," as the saying goes, "fails like success." Nothing is more likely to go wrong, it seems, than something that has gone right.

"Our biggest job of late," one executive put it, "is to avoid what we've become." "We're inbred," another executive declared. "We feed on our own thinking."

Many organizations sense they are in similar situations—death spirals—but have no good ideas for getting out. "Knee-jerk reactions, yes," one manager explains. "But good ideas, no." "We're at the point," another executive adds, when "all the common wisdom is no longer of any real use." Like a lot of managers, he hears the phrases, "work smarter, not harder," "create your future," "thrive on chaos," "teach the elephant to dance." All to no avail. However valid these ideas and strategies may sound, in practice they end up as little more than jingoistic and unfocused reactions. Like a fish in the bottom of a boat, the organization is floundering, and no amount of impassioned flopping will get it out.

Now the organization needs the precious commodity of perspective. The organization and its people need to step back and see where they are. They need to take the first step in the change process: answer the questions, "What happened?" or "What's happening?"

There are a number of models that enable organizations to address this question and establish a context for understanding change. In the book *Aftershock*, Steve Buchholz and I drew on the transformation theory model known as the Growth Curve. Specifically, we used that model as it is described by George Land in his book *Grow or Die*[1] and further developed in his recent book with Beth Jarman, *Breakpoint and Beyond*.[2] As his first book's title suggests, Land's point is simply that growth is natural and change is inevitable. He explains that the growth and change process proceeds first from formation to stability and then, in continuing cycles, back and forth between transformation and stability. Moreover, Land's model is totally consistent with the idea of paradigms and paradigm shifts, all of which make the model quite useful and versatile. I've used the model extensively in my own consulting practice over the years, with great success—until recently.

It all started a few years ago. The model, which had worked so well and been so useful, wasn't generating the same kind of power and buy-in as before. It wasn't that people didn't accept its basic premise. They did. But it no longer seemed to describe their experience. I tried varying my presentation a little, with no success. I began wondering what would I do if this model, arguably one of the best and certainly the simplest context piece I knew of, became useless. And I kept on worrying until I realized that the joke was on me. The model, which had worked so well, was merely obeying its own law. It was starting to *not* work well.

What follows is a brief summary of what the model is changing *from* and what it may be changing *to*. I will briefly review the growth curve itself (in its classical form) and then relate what my experiences with organizations and people in change tell me is a better and certainly more challenging, albeit at times less comforting, model.

THE GROWTH CURVE

The growth curve is a three-stage model that describes the cycle of growth and change. Its primary source is the field of general systems science, and in that context it is used to describe the growth of any system, whether it be biological, organizational, interpersonal, political, or historical. Thus, the model and its methods could be used to describe the growth of a personal relationship, a product life cycle, the history of Russia, or what happened to the dinosaurs. Here we use it to describe what is happening in organizations.

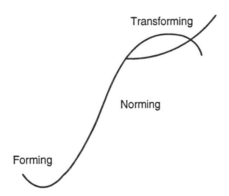

The "Forming" Stage

The "forming" or formative stage of an organization is that time when the organization comes into being. All organizations can trace their origin to a particular date or year. But since that time there have probably been added new divisions, new products, new departments, and the like, each of which had its own start-up date. Therefore, in an organizational setting, formative is synonymous with start-up.

The experience of living in (and through) this start-up period is a mixture of positive and negative. On the positive side, there is excitement, energy, hope, and a sense of mission and possibility. On the negative side, there is anxiety (will we make it?), frustration, false starts, and a sense of taking three steps forward, two steps back. The activities in this period include planning, trial and error, staffing, and trying to allocate resources. In all, the organization is hanging in the balance, hoping that the needle will end up on the positive side.

This stage can be summarized in terms of three key indicators:

Its *mistakes:*	Mistakes are accepted; they are not called mistakes but rather learning.
Its *creativity:*	Creativity and innovation are not only welcomed but vitally necessary. Whatever product or service the organization intends to create doesn't exist yet, so any ideas about it have a palpability they will never have again. The organization is open to new suggestions and ideas, not only about its proposed product or service, but about anything at all that will help the organization grow.
Its *goal:*	The goal of the formative stage is to get out of it—as quickly as possible. The organization may in later years wax nostalgic about the good old days, the fun and the crazy things; but during this formative stage the goal is to find a pattern, get a system in place, get up and running.

The "Norming" Stage

If the upstart organization survives its forming stage, it moves into the "norming" or normative stage. This stage also has positive and negative aspects, but of a different kind. The activities in this stage include fine-tuning, consolidating, writing policies and procedures, and initiating management structures and chains of command. The predominant feelings and outcomes are achievement, predictability, profitability, and a sense of pride. The energy level tends to be lower in this stage, and there are the beginnings of complacency, organizational politics, and even boredom.

The organization begins to struggle with the question, "Are we in a groove or in a rut?" Also, the nature of the three indicators has changed:

Its *mistakes:* Now mistakes are just that—mistakes. The organization has a policy and procedures manual, and if you make a mistake, there is a price to pay.

Its *creativity:* Creativity and innovation are now verbally supported but tacitly discouraged. Creativity is put on a pedestal as something to admire but not to actually practice. Anybody who wants to be creative had better do it according to normative rules. "I don't mind creativity," one manager told me, "just so long as it's on time and within budget." In general, creativity tends to be relegated to certain people and departments, such as R & D. The job of the organization, however, is to accomplish tasks.

Its *goal:* The goal of the normative stage is, quite simply, to stay there.

Thus, the goal of the forming stage is to get to the norming stage, and the goal of the norming stage is to stay there. Some would like to draw the growth curve as a process that reaches the norming stage as quickly as possible and stays there for infinity.

However unrealistic, that notion was accepted in the United States until relatively recently. In general terms, the United States achieved a sense of normalcy around the turn of the century. Traditionally labeled by historians as the "Progressive Era," the period from around 1880 to 1910 is depicted as "America's Coming of Age." Emerging from the Civil War and reconstruction, the nation pulled itself together, we are told, and rushed through the

"Gay 90s" into the new century. It was the era of monopolies and robber barons. It was a "bully" time with a convenient symbol in the form of the rough-riding Teddy Roosevelt. Other observers take a different view, however. They suggest that a more accurate term for this era might be the "reductive era." In his study of this period, *The Search for Order*, historian Robert Wiebe characterizes the era as one of people wanting to settle down and normalize.[3] Wiebe sees it as a time of insecurity, a transition period of anxious consolidation and a striving for predictability. Whatever the cause, the results were impressive. The steel, railroad, timber, financial, communications, automotive, utility, electrical, and petroleum industries—all the major industries—got their foothold in this era. From that point on, the United States moved into a growth mode that survived, in succession, war, prosperity, the Great Depression, and another war to emerge in the 50s—with its factories unscathed and strengthened by war—to take a dominant role in the world. Many organizations had 50, 60, or 70 years of uninterrupted growth; they employed third- and fourth-generation workers. There was no reason to believe that this growth would not continue unabated and that we would not continue to dominate in the automotive, steel, electronics, and telecommunications industries. Then, in the 60s and 70s, quietly, the system began to age. Its challengers—both domestic and foreign—began to grow. Not until the 80s did the real effects of this changing environment begin to make themselves felt. But when they did, we began to experience what the growth curve model calls the transforming stage.

The Transforming Stage

Up to this point, the growth curve model is nothing more than common sense. A system moves from formative beginnings to achieve a sense of normalcy and predictability. At that point in the process, however, the model begins to exert its thesis: that no system, no matter how stable, can continue indefinitely. Sooner or later, as the flattening in the curve indicates, the system will peak, become less effective, and if something isn't done, begin to die.

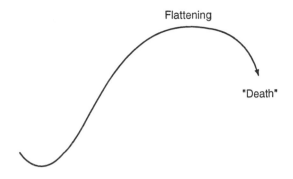

This flattening of the curve is the point when the product (which has dominated the market) begins to lose its market share, when the marriage begins to fail, when the government ceases to function adequately, when the organism ceases to adapt, and when the organization begins to see a decline in profits, quality, customer base, or morale.

At this point the natural instinct of systems in general and organizations in particular is to react and attempt to artificially extend its life. The most common reactions include:

Cuts	Make reductions in money, resources, and/or people. Belt-tightening sets in.
Blame	Find out who made bad decisions and get rid of them.
Denial	Declare that it isn't happening; that the problem is just an anomaly and will correct itself.
Back to basics	Combine cuts and denial; an assertion that if we just get back to what we do best and divest ourselves of certain encumbrances we've taken on, all will return to normal.
Reorganization	Get rid of one regime and replace it with another.
Cure-alls	Introduce a new program or system as a panacea to solve the problem.

Although they vary widely in their techniques, all of these re-actions have one thing in common: they all insist that "This isn't happening! It isn't real! It doesn't have to happen. It will go away if we just take some focused action!" However the problem doesn't go away. It only gets worse. At that point, the response to the flattening turns from reactive to creative. People begin to face the reality of the situation and begin to build a new system which can be represented by a new spur coming off the existing curve. This spur is, of course, the beginning of a new stage or phase of development. Over time, then, the growth of an organization would be a series of interlocking phases.

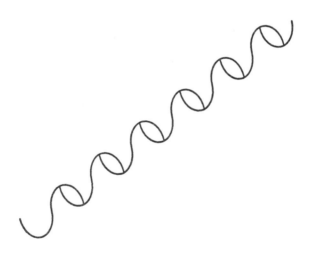

The activities present in this new spur or branch will begin to resemble those of the formative stage: creativity, experimenta-tion, frustration, and a high level of energy. However, it would be inaccurate to call this phase a formative or new formative stage because it does not exist in a vacuum; rather, it has to share the environment with the existing, albeit dying, normative system. As a result, this stage is called the transforming, or sometimes the integrative, stage because the organization is integrating one system out and another in. Whatever the name, this stage is one of replacing the old with the new.

In all, the growth curve is a simple and flexible way to describe the growth of an organization. In my consulting work, I introduce this model to organizations and then ask people to use it to describe their own experiences, either by locating themselves on the curve or by actually drawing the curve in such a way as to chart their history. By comparing the locations chosen or the configuration of their drawings over the past nine years, I have noticed two major trends.

The first trend: Transformative bunching. In the mid-1980s, in response to the question, where is your company or where is your department on the curve, we tended to get little x's all the way up and down the curve. Most were located in the normative area, and there was a general trend of movement toward the transformative area. By the late 80s and early 90s, however, this pattern had changed rather dramatically. The x's were clustered toward the top of the curve in the late normative and early transformative stages. Indeed, when I ask for locations today, it comes off as a rhetorical question. The people look at me as if to say, "Well, isn't it obvious? We're in the transformative stage." At that point we talk about *where* in the transformative stage they perceive themselves to be. There are six general choices.

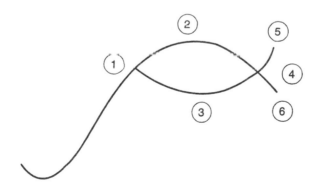

1. Knocking on the Door—just entering the third stage.
2. Hanging On—trying to preserve the old order.
3. Branching Off—trying new ideas and procedures.

4. Reaching the Crossroads—the make-or-break point for our
   new ideas and procedures.
5. Consolidating—beginning to normalize the changes.
6. Dying on the Vine—inability to make the transition.

Most common are positions one, two and three; position four
is the next most popular; position five is commonly described as
"Well, that's where upper management thinks we are"; position
six, though not uncommon, is usually suggested in hushed tones
from the back of the room.

The basic conclusion to be drawn is that people perceive themselves to be in a state of change; they no longer argue or insist
that things are still normal. However obvious that statement may
sound, it is a major shift from just a few years ago. Then, it was
common to hear people try to hang on to their sense that things
were still normal. Now, people are beginning to take change seriously as an issue that needs to be addressed rather than something that will eventually go away or slow down.

Still, there are those who will argue, "But haven't we always
had change? I don't see how the current changes are any different." Their point is well taken. Change itself is nothing new. But
is this current change somehow different? In other words, has
change changed? Charles Handy, in *The Age of Unreason*, writes:
"The changes are different this time: They are discontinuous and
not part of a pattern."[4] I believe Handy is correct, that change has
changed. But to many people these statements sound like just so
much theory and word play. They need something concrete in
their own experience to convince them.

   Broken boxes. One of the simplest and most powerful
ways I have found to make the case that the changes are different
this time is the analogy of the broken box. The idea came to me as
a result of a casual comment once made by a manager who said,
"You know, I don't mind change just so long as you don't alter
anything." She delivered the statement with a straight face, completely unaware of the irony of her statement. Because of her se-
riousness, I tried to understand what she meant, and came up
with this. Imagine the current systems (normative) as a box; and
change as the arrows within that box.

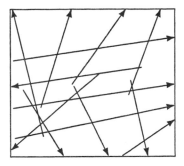

This manager was saying that she had a lot of irritating, constant, and disruptive changes to contend with. Her comment, "I don't mind change just so long as you don't alter anything," was her way of saying, "I can handle the changes; just don't break the box." As long as change is limited to exceptions and alterations within the box, we can maintain some measure of control. I find that people who consider themselves old hands at change usually refer to changes within the box. What has now happened—or better, what people finally realize—is that the box has been broken.

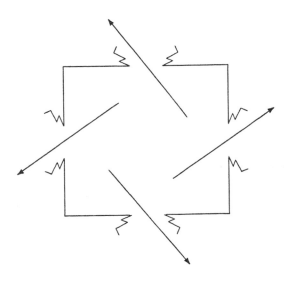

Their systems, their hierarchies, their markets, even their basic assumptions about their work and direction, have been exploded. On the surface, we see mergers, buyouts, reorganizations, shifting markets, competition, deregulation, and layoffs. Under the surface are the deeper issues of personal loss: loss of control, loss of relationships, loss of competence, and loss of identity. Change is no longer a matter of dealing with exceptions, putting out fires, or incorporating new developments into an existing system. Rather, it is understanding and establishing a new context—a new box—and trying to figure out how it works. When people whose boxes have been broken recall what they used to call change, they say, "Those changes were peanuts compared to what we're up against now." And they ask, "Will things return to normal?"

The answer to this question is important and more fundamental. In its ideal form, the growth curve predicts that after the transformative phase you will return to another period of normalcy. That's where the growth curve breaks down.

The second trend: No normative stage. My argument has now come full circle. When people get hit by change, the first thing they want is perspective. The growth curve is a simple, effective model to do that job, but lately, the model doesn't seem to be working as well as it had and may itself be changing. About a year ago I was presenting this model to a group of executives. They seemed interested and were using the growth curve lingo to describe their experiences. Finally, one of them said, "You know, this is a nice model and it makes sense, but I'm not sure if it really describes our company." Others concurred.

"Well," I responded, "the model is not meant to be prescriptive but descriptive. In other words, it's not supposed to tell you what will happen as much as give you a way to describe what's happening." At that point he looked at the magic marker in my hand and asked "May I?"

"By all means," I said.

The executive then proceeded to draw the history of his company, using the growth curve. With a little editing and some fictional model numbers, this is basically what he said:

Our first stage of growth was from about 1968 to 1976 with the model 111.

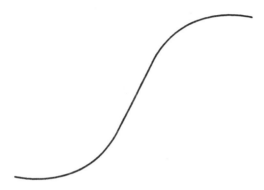

Then as sales of that model flattened, we went to model 222. That stage only lasted four years.

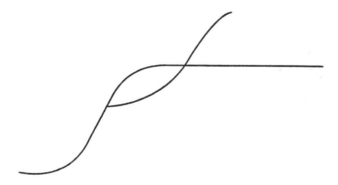

Then some new technology came in—quickly—after only a couple of years, and the model 222 started a slow decline as we ramped up for the 333, which was really just a souped-up 222.

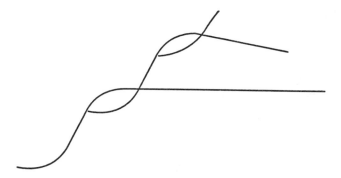

From then on it was one change after another. And they all came in before the previous one had even matured or even got close to normalcy. And it's been like that ever since.

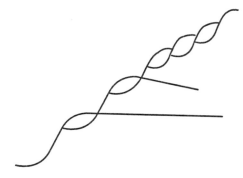

In a stylized form, he had redrawn the growth curve. In this

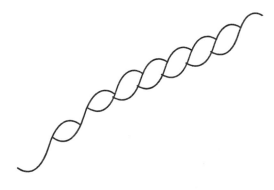

new configuration, there are no normative periods. Although there are succeeding developments, the overall effect of the new configuration is one of a permanent transformative stage. To understand this development, another, and related, model of change describes the change process in terms of: freeze, unfreeze and re-freeze. This model refers to the process of planned change in which one begins with a stable (i.e., frozen) system. The plan then is to unfreeze and reform it, and then re-freeze it again. The model describes a simple normative–transformative–normative progression. In its middle stage the system is liquid. This liquid state is transitory and basically undesirable. The skills needed are those of re-forming and re-freezing. But what if the system were to remain liquid permanently? Then instead of the skills of re-freezing, the skills needed might become those of floating, navigating, and observing. The diagram the man had drawn, then, was of an organization in permanent liquidity.

The rest of the executives in the room agreed and were quick to recognize that what he had drawn was a perfect graphic representation of change as permanent white water. No longer do people talk about *a change* or *the change*; rather, they speak generically of change: an ongoing series of alterations and disruptions. Add to this the fact that the box has been broken and the result is an environment that calls for a very different way of operating. At this point, I began to take chaos seriously.

CHAOS

At the general level, *chaos* is the colloquial term of preference, as in Tom Peters' *Thriving on Chaos*, to describe the turbulent environment we are currently living in. Technically, chaos refers to what is called "nonlinear dynamics": complex and inherently unpredictable, but not random, phenomena. In other words, the study of chaotic behavior asserts that what may appear on the surface to be random and chaotic may have an underlying order which, if discerned, can lead to new and more creative directions and solutions. In his book, *Chaos: Making a New Science*, James Gleick introduces the reading public to this field of scientific study which focuses on what he terms "the universal behavior of complexity."[5] Simply defined, the study of chaos, instead of focusing on "the analysis of systems in terms of their constituent parts," focuses instead on patterns in a seemingly random flow. However, discerning these patterns and connections requires a new mindset and a new set of skills. In his application of chaos theory to organizations, Ralph Stacey, in *Managing the Unknowable*, explains the difference between the old and the new, as follows:

> Most western managers believe that long-term success flows from a state of stability, harmony, predictability, discipline and consensus . . . *stable equilibrium.*

He goes on to say that recent discoveries have shown that stable equilibrium is not a useful framework for understanding complex systems.

> Rather, these discoveries have revealed that the continuous creativity found in natural systems is driven by stable laws that generate specific kinds of instability within recognizable patterns . . . *bounded instability.*[6]

The purpose of the remainder of this chapter is to show to what extent the principles of chaos study may help us in understanding organizational change. Having said this, I need to raise a caution. I have read too much of organizational theory, sociology, and history that try to force-fit scientific principles to organizational or social phenomena. Everything from "Social Darwinism" to entropy to relativity to Heisenberg's Uncertainty Principle have been brought to bear at one time or another in simplistic and often misleading ways. So the question becomes, can the study of chaos be applied directly to organizations, or is it just an analogy? Stacey argues the former, stating that "nonlinear dynamics and chaotic behavior apply literally to human business systems; they are not simply an analogy or a metaphor." I have neither the background nor the inclination to extend Stacey's direct applications. But believing that those applications do go beyond analogy and metaphor, I have chosen here to take the middle road. I will focus on some of the key principles of chaos theory and demonstrate how they can be applied in a very real way to both understand and cope with a changing environment.

Our starting point is Stacey's notion that Western managers tend to operate from the assumption that success flows from a state of stable equilibrium. I would add that our current reliance on linear systems thinking is now beginning to interfere with our ability to change. To explain this idea more fully we need to consider what might be called the "power of paradigm." A paradigm is simply a model, a way of explaining reality. The Ptolomaic paradigm of the sun and planets rotating around the earth was the dominant paradigm for centuries until Copernicus demonstrated that the earth and other planets actually rotate around the sun. The concept of the paradigm is very popular today. People speak of paradigm shifts and paradigm paralysis with ease. The terms have become standard parts of organizational and management lingo.

The deeper power of paradigms, however, is captured in Thomas Kuhn's statement that "To reject one paradigm without simultaneously substituting another is to reject science itself."[7] In other words—don't get caught without some paradigm, otherwise you'll be considered unscientific.

Why? one might ask. Why, if one system clearly isn't working, does one necessarily have to have another system to take its place? The legacy of the Newtonian revolution and the resulting quest for predictable, consistent, scientific systems seems to have fostered a belief that to be left without a system is terrible. If Kuhn is right, then to be scientific and truly modern it is better to have a bad paradigm than no paradigm at all. And that seems to be what is happening. Our current systems aren't working and there don't seem to be any other systems standing ready to take their places. As a result, people and organizations are clamoring after ready-made systems.

A good example of this system-seeking is the current popularity of total quality management. The TQM techniques and applications I have seen and worked with are valid and useful. What interests me more, however, is not the systems themselves but the beliefs about the systems. One person explained it this way: "When the Japanese were down and hurting, trying to catch up, they used these techniques to improve themselves. Now that we're down and hurting we can use the same techniques to pull ourselves up and be a world leader again."

Probably not too many people accept the idea that a new system can solve all our problems. But there is a tendency in our organizations to avoid being caught without a system. I believe that TQM is certainly a valuable tool, but not a panacea. It is not the system that can automatically create a new era of normative growth. In sum, all of these trends—hanging on to old and dying systems, grasping at new, ready-made systems and valuing new systems or approaches beyond their ability to deliver—are, as means to deal with change, temporary at best.

Just as science has done, organizations are discovering that the systems or phenomena they are trying to control or describe are much more complex than they thought. They are also beginning to suspect that the control they thought they had in the past may have been to some degree an illusion. And this is where chaos comes in.

TAKING CHAOS SERIOUSLY

Organizations today, and the implied set of rules by which they seem to operate, no longer work as well as before. But what's worse is that their traditional coping techniques don't work either. These coping mechanisms, expressed so eloquently in phrases such as damage control and putting out fires were in-box solutions. That is, the solutions assumed the system, or box, was still intact and that the changes were merely exceptions within the four walls. Now that the box is either broken or breaking, organizations are faced with chaos, a seemingly random environment in which older assumptions are prone to shorter and shorter half lives.

In their panic, managers are calling for, and at times grasping at, new systems to solve their problems. What they are beginning to realize, at a tactical rather than just a rhetorical level, is that if they can't have a new system, at the very least they need a new point of view and an attendant set of rudimentary skills. The study of chaos may have something to offer.

One of the clearest exponents of the basics of chaos theory is one Dr. Ian Malcolm. Malcolm is the fictional creation of Michael Crichton, in his sci-fi thriller *Jurassic Park*. Dr. Malcolm is the brilliant but arrogant, irritatingly accurate mathematician—the character we love to hate—who serves as the author's mouthpiece for chaos theory. Although certainly not an authoritative source, Malcolm's comments manage to catch the flavor of chaos theory in a way that is understandable.

Malcolm explains, "If you knew enough you could predict anything. That's been a cherished scientific belief since Newton." He adds, "Ever since Newton and Descartes, science has explicitly offered us a vision of total control." Concluding, he loftily declares, "And now chaos theory proves that unpredictability is built into our daily lives. It is as mundane as the rainstorm we cannot predict. And so the grand vision of science, hundreds of years old—the dream of total control—has died in our century."[8]

The novel itself presents an intriguing story about a multimillionaire who funds the cloning and genetic engineering of dinosaurs, and then buys an island off the coast of Costa Rica to set up his Jurassic Park. His plan is to create a clean, well-lighted dinosaur park for fun and profit for the children and large investors of the world. His dinosaurs are isolated on this island, separated by fences and genetically engineered to be both sterile and dependent on the substance lysine. The plan seems foolproof; the system is up and running. But then, in accordance with Dr. Malcolm's relentless logic, the whole system begins to go chaotic. The sterile dinosaurs show a marked ability to breed, they seem to be outgrowing their lysine dependency, they break down the fences, and they finally begin to migrate to the mainland.

As I read Crichton's novel, I pondered the implications. Was this a cautionary tale? Was it about genetic engineering, or maybe science in general, or perhaps human organizations, or even a parable about America and globalism? Certainly the basic elements invite speculation. Large, powerful, isolated, separately organized, supposedly sterile, supposedly dependent but actually adaptable and lusty creatures suddenly breaking down all the barriers and running amuck. Somehow, it sounded familiar.

Lest the entire chaos scenario sound too doom and gloom, however, Malcolm also points up the deeper nature of his brave new world.

"So chaos is all just random and unpredictable?" one character asks him.

"No," Malcolm replies. "We actually find hidden regularities within the complex variety of a system's behavior. That's why chaos has now become a very broad theory that's used to study everything from the stock market, to rioting crowds, to brain waves during epilepsy. Any sort of complex system where there is confusion and unpredictability. We can find an underlying order."[9]

As the (real) physicist Paul Davies explains:

> Thus although chaotic behavior is, by definition, dauntingly difficult to model, there is still some underlying order in its manifestation, and we may obtain a broad understanding of the principles that govern this particular form of complexity.[10]

So at its most fundamental level, chaos does not throw out systems or principles or even paradigms. It merely suggests that those systems are far more complex than we thought, and further, that when the speed of the system's development picks up, what appeared stable now appears chaotic. But there ultimately is order, the argument goes; a deeper, underlying order too complex to be caught by the level of our current linear thinking. There are also principles and skills and applications. None of the rigor of science is left behind; rather, it is now applied in new directions. The question is: "What new directions?"

In a stable or relatively stable environment, the target is, as the saying goes, standing still. Thus we analyze the system in question and develop a plan to address it. In a white-water environment, we are dealing with an evolving and elusive moving target. Thus, our ability to analyze it is limited. Because we are caught in the midst of a flow, we have no clear idea of how or where it started. In short, we have no sense of what are called initial conditions. As Davies puts it:

> The problem comes when we try to specify those initial conditions. Obviously in practice we can never know exactly the state of a system at the outset. However refined our observations are, there will always be some error involved.[11]

As a consequence, the sacrosanct skills of normalcy fail us when we feel we need them most. In response to a chaotic system, Davies goes on to explain:

Gathering more information about the system will not eliminate [its randomness]. Whereas in an ordinary system . . . the calculations keep well ahead of the action, in a chaotic system more and more information must be processed to maintain the same level of accuracy, and the calculation can barely keep pace with the actual events. In other words, all power of prediction is lost.[12]

In our current environment, then, we are truly living on the edge. Our information gathering and planning models can't keep up. To help ourselves, we have to first recognize and admit that we are no longer what we used to describe as in control. We have to stand up, in essence, and declare (in the style of a struggling substance abuser) "Hi, my name is Pat and I'm a control junkie." Having confessed our habit, we are free to explore a new dimension. As Davies concludes:

Although the word *chaos* implies something negative and destructive, there is a creative aspect to it too. The random element endows a chaotic system with a certain freedom to explore a vast range of patterns."[13]

In short, we are free to approach what are known in chaos circles as "strange attractors."

"Strange Attractors"

One of the contributions of chaos theory is the wonderful term *strange attractor*. To understand this term, we first have to understand what a real attractor is. A real attractor is simply the point to which a system is going. If you shoot an artillery shell, and you know all the data regarding mass of the projectile, angle of the cannon, power of the charge, and wind direction, you can pretty well determine where the projectile will land. The point where it will land is the attractor. This system can be represented linearly as follows:

Starting Point: Attractor:
(the cannon)   (where the projectile lands)

In so-called Newtonian physics, attractors are known. Scientific laws are based on (or better, are the expression of) known real attractors. Chaotic systems, by contrast, don't have real attractors. That is why they are called chaotic. Far from being totally random and unpredictable, however, these systems have strange attractors. Strange attractors are points toward which systems seem to be going but never get there because something else happens. In what has become one of the icons of chaos theory, the Lorenz attractor or the "Lorenz Mask" illustrates this idea.[14] The figure is a computer image of the hidden structure within a disorderly stream of data.

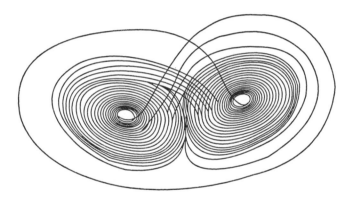

The two eyes on the Lorenz Mask are the strange attractors, the points to which the system appears to be going. Unlike the diagram for the real attractor, this diagram does not describe a straight line but a figure 8. If you are traveling on that line you may appear at first to be going somewhere, but soon you find yourself doubling back. You may perceive the figure eight pattern after a while, or you may not. You may just experience it as going around in circles or going nowhere. To illustrate the idea of strange attractors, imagine the following situation in your organization: a couple of people come to you, really steamed, complaining about some things going on in the department. You can see they are upset so you decide to apply a linear problem-solving model you learned in a recent workshop. The principles of: clarify the issue, legitimize the feelings, seek creative solutions, and the like are floating in your head. So you begin. But your attempts seem futile. The people are really angry; the confrontation is all over the map. Every time you seem to clarify an issue it—and you—are abruptly dismissed. The discussion has gone chaotic: seemingly random and out of control.

After finally giving up and just listening for a while, you begin to notice that five issues seem to be repeating themselves. There even seems to be some order or connection to the five but you're not sure. But there are five issues to which the confrontation gravitates. These are the strange attractors in the chaotic conversation. At first, they seemed random and unrelated. But as some connections are seen, you begin to discern patterns. Now how do you deal with this chaos?

If you decide to go straight for issue A to clarify and solve it, you're likely to get B, C, D, and E thrown in your face. That kind of linear approach probably won't work because you don't know yet if A, or any other single issue, is the central issue. There may not even be a *key* issue. Maybe they are all indicators of a root issue, such as respect or trust. In any case, you will not know until you abandon your add-water-and-stir problem-solving methodology and begin to apply chaos skills, such as observation and testing connections. Things may then clear up a little, causing the chaotic system to settle down and even be more open, eventually, to the problem-solving skills you had just abandoned.

This is a simple example of the challenges presented by chaotic behavior. It is also an example of looking for and testing strange attractors. James Gleick writes of the first chaos theorists that, "They had an eye for pattern . . . They had a taste for randomness and complexity, for jagged edges and sudden leaps . . . They feel they are turning back a trend toward reductionism: the analysis of systems in terms of their constituent parts . . . They believe that they are looking for the whole."[15]

Clearly, the specific skills and tasks of chaos scientists go far beyond Gleick's poetic description, just as the tasks of people caught in organizational chaos go beyond writing vision statements and reading *Megatrends*. But for both groups, the fundamental challenge is the need to experiment and apply while at the same time trying to discern and direct.

The primary differentiators between a stable environment and a chaotic environment are:

Stable environment

Assumes an underlying order from which principles can be drawn.

Attempts to reduce principles to stable, predictable applications

Focuses on real attractors.

Values infinite data; can operate with prescribed amounts of data; prefers to avoid risks or blind experimentation if possible.

Tends to work forward from theories or hypotheses.

Makes long-range plans.

Chaotic environment

Assumes an underlying order from which principles may or may not emerge.

Attempts to discern patterns and trends for possible future applications.

Focuses on real attractors if possible, but is sensitive to and seeks out strange attractors.

Values data; often does not get enough data to operate with full assurance and must therefore take more risks and experiment more.

Tends to work backwards from results and observations.

Projects long-term outcomes but makes short-term plans.

CONCLUSION

The purpose of this chapter has been to provide an expanded context for understanding change. We have used models, metaphors, scientific comparisons, and the experiences of people caught in the change process.

To begin, we described pictures, drawn by people on the receiving end of disruptive change, and their varied expressions of aimlessness, abandonment, and ignorance. Next, we looked at a model for organizational growth and change—the Growth Curve. We then discussed how this model was basically obeying its own precepts and beginning to not work as well as it had in the past. Specifically, on the testimony of a number of executives, managers, and workers, it appears that because of the speed and complexity of the changes that organizations are facing, the formative, normative, and transformative stages are constantly overlapping, creating permanent phase-three conditions— permanent white water—that is, a chaotic environment.

Finally, we drew on the ideas and language of what some call the emerging science of chaos. In summarizing, it is important to cut through the particulars of the discussion and focus on two main points:

1. We seem to be heir to a three- to four-hundred-year-old intellectual tradition that sought to create a sense of control through the evolution of laws and systems. However useful and beneficial this has been for our scientific advancement and quality of life, it has also led us to become too reliant on linear systems, resulting in a sense of panic when our current systems no longer work and we don't have other systems to replace them.

2. Just as there are skills and techniques available to run stable systems, so too there are skills and techniques for operating in a chaotic environment. Many of these skills and techniques are the same as those needed in a stable environment. There are others, however, that are quite different and which contain a large attitudinal component. They can be summarized briefly as:

   a. The ability to perceive is more important initially than the ability to plan.
   b. Intuition may initially be more useful than deduction.
   c. Organizations and people may have to act on what a stable system would consider insufficient information.
   d. The ability to control one's own tension is elevated to the level of a survival skill.

Although the historical argument regarding our reliance on systems may seem somewhat academic or esoteric, I think what one organizational change expert has labeled the human addiction to control (our faith that there will always be systems to guide us) cannot be underestimated. In the past this belief led us to think we were in control when we really were not; and in the future, if not relinquished, it will block our ability to cope with chaos. Once we accept not having that kind of assurance, the second main point and its four general suggestions begin to seem more realistic. These so-called chaos skills, when separated from the scientific and organizational overlay, begin to look suspiciously like fundamental survival and creativity skills.

Finally, one of the clearest examples of this point of view (regarding creativity and survival) appeared in a *Science News* article entitled "Crazy Rhythms," a report about complexity and chaos in the human heart.[16] When a heart ceases its normal rhythm and beats irregularly, there is obvious cause for concern. But are these irregular variations in heartbeat random, or are they chaotic? That is, do they exhibit a deeper pattern? These are questions that heart researchers are asking themselves, because while random heartbeats spell trouble, chaotic heartbeats could provide clues to the way the heart may be coping with its own problem.

Standard procedure would dictate that a variability in heartbeat calls for measures from medication to the electric shock pads to get the heartbeat back to normal. The loss of certain kinds of variability or complexity in heartbeats may not be wise, however. The article reports that in some of their studies, Harvard researchers Ary Goldberger and his colleagues, "found that a loss of complexity in the heartbeat pattern precedes sudden death." The article continues, "This variability, he [Goldberger] suggests, gives a living, dynamic system, such as the heart, the robustness it requires to cope with change." Thus, instead of being a sign of impending doom, chaotic behavior is the system's creative means for coping with the changes it is undergoing. And conversely, trying to regulate a chaotic system may have the effect of killing it.

My own experience in organizations tends to support the view that, as Stacey puts it, "we would expect to find that companies fail when they get close to equilibrium states." Too many times I have observed that when organizations encounter change and begin to experience variations ("corporate fibrillations") they react by immediately baring the corporate chest and applying the shock pads in an attempt to jump-start the organization back to normal. In so doing, they often short-circuit the creative behavior that may have saved the patient. Goldberger's statement that chaotic variations may give a system the "robustness" it requires to cope with change says clearly that bounded instability, not equilibrium, is the way through.

Finally, chaotic states are by their nature inherently creative. Quoting Stacey again:

> In chaos then, creativity is a potentially ongoing process that is internally generated in a spontaneous manner. It is neither proaction

according to some prior design nor reaction to environmental change, but rather continuing interaction with other systems in the environment. A system in this state creates its own environment and its own future.[17]

The remainder of this book is a fuller examination of the basic skills needed to establish and support an organization which is resilient to change and able to capitalize on its own chaotic variations.

Chapter Two

Equipment Check: Skills for a New Context

Learn how to choose.

Alvin Toffler

For a lot of people, coping with change is like trying to find their way around a new city with a map of their old city.

Anonymous

If there is anything I can't stand, it's intolerance!

I once worked with an organization whose CEO was convinced that an "enabling" leadership model was better than the autocratic model, and took the opportunity one day to address a group of about 25 employees to emphasize his commitment to this point of view.

He was a tall, imposing man with a resonant voice. He was also an eccentric of sorts; he wore a broad Stetson hat and often espoused refreshing noncorporate views. "Fear," he said, "was the enemy of good leadership," adding, "There will be no more fear in this organization." "In fact," he concluded, projecting forcefully into the employees' faces, "my goal is to **drive fear out of this organization!**" Shuddering and cowering in their chairs, the employees fearfully nodded their agreement. Later, to his credit, he was able to see the humor in his presentation and laugh at himself. "But I feel so strongly about it," he explained, "it's difficult not to get enthusiastic."

What interests me most about this story and ones like it is what I like to call the war of the worlds. People and organizations often have a fairly good idea of the general direction they want to go but lack the skills and attitudes to get there. As a result, they tend by inertia to take sides with the very things they're trying to get rid of. And they find themselves involved in contradictory activities such as resolving to get rid of autocratic behavior by autocratically rooting it out. Or, as related, the CEO's efforts to rid people of their fear in fact scared them to death. In these situations, people become like the proverbial leader who says: "We need to get rid of intolerance because if there's anything I can't stand, it's intolerance."

Today, people and organizations find themselves in situations similar to the era of the horseless carriage. Generally, people tend to describe the new in terms of the known. Therefore the automobile, when first introduced, could not attain an identity of its own because of the greater familiarity with what it was replacing: the carriage. So for a while it was a horseless carriage. Eventually it was able to take on an identity of its own. Similarly, the first radios went through a wireless stage. In organizations today we run into similar terms, such as "leaderless teams." We also have hierarchical (pyramidal) structures which are being flattened or inverted. It seems we can't quite live without that pyramid, but since it isn't working for us, let's squeeze it or turn it upside down. Eventually, we will be able to throw away the pyramid altogether; to move from our own horseless-carriage stage and see what we have become.

In the meantime, however, we need to keep moving forward. In that spirit, this chapter addresses three issues:

1. The nature of the system we are moving from compared to the nature of the environment we are moving to.
2. The main obstacles that stand in our way.
3. The basic skills needed by organizations wishing to make that transition.

A COMPARISON OF ATTITUDES

In Chapter 1 we established that many organizations today are not only in the transformative stage of their evolution, but in perpetual transformation—permanent white water; and when an organization and people find themselves in this state, a fundamentally different set of skills and assumptions is necessary. Recognizing, much less practicing, these chaos skills will undoubtedly be hampered by the horseless-carriage syndrome. Therefore, in an attempt to point the way toward the future, we need see the basic needs of this new environment as compared to those of the older, more stable environment.

I commonly ask groups I work with to first answer these two questions:

1. What do people in a normative, or stable, environment want?
2. What is the job of a manager or leader in a stable environment?

The lists they produce generally come out as follows:

In a Stable Environment

People's wants.   People in a stable environment want:

Security	Clear directions
Predictability	Recognition
Stability	Opportunity
Better salary	Creativity
Perks	

The items almost always fall in that order. People first want the box: a stable, clear, and secure environment. Even entrepreneurial types who supposedly thrive on chaos want that chaos to remain inside acceptable limits of change. Having established a base, the next questions are: "What's in it for me? I've been a good and loyal employee, I've put in my time." "How about a better salary, a little incentive, some perks?" And also, "How about some recognition for a job well done?" Lastly, there are requests for creativity and opportunity. But not too much, we might caution. We don't want to go outside the box, but "what kind of fun things or growth opportunities are there within the system?" Although this list of wants may appear somewhat conservative and even dull, life in a well-functioning normative system can be very fulfilling and rewarding.

In a Stable Environment

Manager's/leader's job.   The job of a supervisor or manager in a stable environment is to:

Plan	Troubleshoot
Organize	Coach and counsel
Manage to specs	Look to the future
Maintain	Be creative
Bolster morale	

This progression is similar to that indicated by the employees' wants. It starts with the bedrock of system maintenance, moves on to the people issues regarding morale and coaching, and finally pays what, too often, is lip service to creativity and future thinking. The list is basically the content for Management 101. The normative manager's function is fundamentally to run, protect, and maintain the existing system. Taken together, the two lists are complementary. The manager-leader's job is essentially to provide and vouchsafe what the people want. Granted there is dissatisfaction within this system, but generally not enough to threaten or change it.

I don't know if a pure normative environment ever really existed, but I do know that it exists in books and also in people's minds. Up until relatively recently our organizations and our culture, in general, have seen themselves as basically stable. Granted there was change, but that change was always held within the secure confines of the existing box.

Once these lists are generated, I ask the group:

1. What do people in a transforming or changing environment want?
2. What is the job of the manager/leader in this environment?

Their responses are telling.

In a Changing Environment

People's wants. People in a changing environment want:

Security	Creativity
Clear direction	Teamwork
Honest	Recognition
Information/	Training
communication	Clear directions (tell me
Support	what you want)
Stability	

Keep in mind that these are the things people say they want, not what someone else thinks they ought to want. Not surprisingly, security heads the list. But next are calls for context: "Tell me what's happening. Give me information. Don't keep me in the dark (or I'll make up my own information and send it back to you via the rumor mill)." Then come the conservative cries: "Tell me what you want" and "Support me"; followed by the more liberated calls for creativity, teamwork, and training; followed again by the conservative appeal for stability. As you can see, the wants in this list have a greater range and in some cases are contradictory. They go from reasonable demands for information to liberated calls for creativity to conservative appeals for stability and security.

I tell groups that while all of these wants are understandable, only some are reasonable. For example, a request for information and communication is both understandable and reasonable. In times of change, organizations have a duty to keep people updated and informed. However, a request for stability and security is understandable but basically unreasonable because it is beyond the power of a boss or even the organization to guaranty continued stability and security. The demand for security, then, is what I would term an "old tape attitude" about change, by which I mean an attitude reasonable in a stable environment, but unrealistic or counterproductive in a changing environment.

In a Changing Environment

Manager's/leader's job. The job of a supervisor or manager in a changing environment includes being a:

Cheerleader	Communicator	Planner
Listener	Father confessor	Experimenter
Innovator	Advocate	Risk taker

Also all of the job functions listed above as duties
of the stable (normative) system's manager/leader.

The list for the change manager is always longer and more diverse than any of the other three lists. I ask the group to look at the change manager's job versus the normative manager's job. Specifically I ask "In what way are the words and terms different?"

The most common responses are that the words on the change manager's list are:

More people oriented.

More energized.

More metaphorical.

More vague.

Express a greater sense of risk.

People themselves have more of a feel for the change manager's job than they have any explicit sense of the tasks and skills. But certainly there is a marked shift in the balance between process and people skills. Whereas in a stable environment the ratio may have been 80 percent process skills (planning, monitoring, etc.) and 20 percent people skills (coaching, counseling, etc.), the ratio in a changing environment may be 50/50. Indeed, at the beginning of a change situation it may even shift for a while to 80 percent people, 20 percent process. (One change manager commented dryly that, "No, at the beginning of the whole thing the ratio was about 80/80.") Whatever the ratio, the primary point is that in times of change, the number and intensity of people issues rises dramatically. Similarly, the nature of the manager's process skills also changes markedly. Whereas the normative manager's job was to run the system, the change manager's job is to tweak it or expand it or reinvent it. The essential differences between the job of the normative manager and that of the change manager can be summarized as follows:

Leader/Manager Skills

Stable Environment

Focus on process skills:
    Analyze
    Plan and inform
    Direct
    Coordinate individual and team action
    Monitor and control

Theme: Planning/Implementation/Control

Changing Environment

Reliance on chaos skills:
    Observe and clarify
    Support

(continued)

Facilitate team problem solving
Trial and error
Share feedback

Theme: Observation/Experimentation/Support

The comparison of the needs and responsibilities of employees and managers in a stable environment versus a changing environment presents a picture of two radically differing cultures.

Stable Environment	*Changing Environment*
1. The structure or system (i.e., the shape of the box) is known. Therefore, communicating exceptions on a need-to-know basis is effective and efficient.	The structure or system is continually changing. Therefore, both tactical and new box configuration information must be communicated regularly. Communicating on a need-to-know basis only fosters distrust and rumors.
2. Satisfaction levels are medium to high. Dissatisfaction is focused on specific issues. Traditional problem-solving techniques work.	Satisfaction levels are medium to low. Dissatisfaction in the form of anxiety is unfocused. Traditional problem-solving techniques don't work.
3. People can reasonably expect security (provided they are willing to accept the organization's employment and salary offers).	People cannot reasonably expect security.
4. Job requirements are clear and are communicated down by management.	Job requirements may fluctuate and must be clarified across by two-way management–employee communication.
5. Risk taking and innovation are not necessary in large degree.	Risk taking and innovation are survival skills but often punished by the existing cultural norms.
6. Emotional issues among people tend to be at a minimum and are viewed as exceptions or problems.	Emotional issues among people tend to be widespread and normal, but need to be addressed.
7. Long-term plans can be set and worked; they can also be adjusted via mid-course corrections.	Long-term plans tend not to work; organizations tend to develop more general goals, develop short-term plans, and revisit their goals often to tweak them given change developments.

ORGANIZATIONAL BLEED THROUGH

The lists and information in this chapter, as well as in the first, have given us basic working knowledge of a stable versus a changing/chaotic environment. For some, it is a restatement of the obvious, for others a new insight, and for still others, a handy synthesis and summary of the basic juxtapositions taking place in the organizational climate today.

Given this context, what obstacles stand in the way of people and organizations accepting and functioning in the new environment? The answer to that is what I call "bleed through": a rule that worked in a normative environment bleeds through (or slips through) and is thereby applied to a changing environment. The best example of this phenomenon occurs in the area of communication. People in a changing environment want information—continuous, candid, and current information. Correspondingly, change managers and leaders agree that ongoing communication is an essential task they must perform. We have therefore a situation in which the managers and employees are in what a friend of mine likes to call violent agreement.

My question to the managers and employees at this point would be: What's going to get in the way? More specifically, what is likely to stop you from doing the very thing you both say you want? The answers come easily:

Time—Everybody is busy enough as it is. We don't have time, or it's not convenient to stop all the time to communicate.

Ignorance—Managers say "I don't have the information." In response, employees often feel that they really do have it but are holding it back.

Sketchy information—Managers have information, but it's incomplete. Employees again feel that management isn't organized.

Anticipated Effect—Managers are wary about giving the information because it may upset employees.

Self-image—Managers worry that providing incomplete, volatile information will upset people and make them look bad, both to employees and management.

Habit—Managers tend to use information judiciously, as a tool. This practice seems to undermine its value.

Lack of Direction—Employees tend to want clear direction. Lack of it creates static.

Given these real culture obstacles, it is no wonder that the communication process everybody heartily endorses never takes place. The force of this real culture speaks in a little voice to managers and employees.

Manager's little voice:

You're gonna do what? You're gonna tell 'em that? Are you crazy? You haven't got time! Besides, if you tell 'em that, you'll only upset them. They're gonna hate you. Not to mention that you don't even know what you're talking about, do you? They'll see right through you. And what about your boss? He's not gonna like what he's seeing. You're gonna lose your job!

The little voice is the pernicious spokesman of what in effect are the following normative rules for managers:

1. Good managers are prepared and they always know what they're talking about. They don't release half-baked information.
2. Good managers don't unduly upset their people.
3. Good managers always provide clear direction.
4. Good managers use information carefully.
5. Good managers are always in control.

The employee's little voice has a somewhat different approach:

Employee's little voice:

Oh sure! That isn't what they told you last week. They're lying! Or else they're holding something back. And how are you supposed to act on that, anyway? Where are the directions? How can they expect you to work if they don't tell you what to do? This person's incompetent—can't be trusted.

The employee's hidden rules are:

1. I should always get clear directions.
2. I should never get contradictory information.

3. I should have enough information to answer all my questions.
4. I should always be comfortable.

For both managers and employees, normative rules and assumptions bled through and negated or stopped the communication process. In most of the organizations I have worked with, the habits of standard operating procedure are largely unspoken, but very firm nevertheless. As a result, very specific old tapes need to be addressed before an organization can deal with change on its own terms. And managers and employees need a corresponding list of good or more useful attitudes. The following charts list the old tapes and suggest new approaches to replace them.

Management Choices

Old Tape	New Approaches
1. **"I should only communicate what I know for sure."** Don't communicate incomplete or potentially changeable information.	Keep people posted as events change. Let them know that you know the information is not as complete or permanent as you would like, but that under the circumstances, it may be more useful.
2. **"I need to set a positive example."** Always put on a confident face.	Let people know how you really feel. If you don't, they will pick it up in different ways. Be honest, but not a victim. Redefine positive not as necessarily happy, but as identifying the best options under the circumstances.
3. **"Information is key."** Just tell people what is going on and they will adjust.	People need both information and empathy during change. You need to listen to and deal with their concerns and worries as well as their information needs.
4. **"I should have a plan."** Managers should have a clear plan for the future.	You might be better off with just an approach or with some possible outcomes and then allow your people, as a team, to develop and implement your plans.
5. **"I'm responsible."** Managers are in charge and responsible for results.	No longer are managers responsible for plans and outcomes. Rather, they are responsible for giving away some of their responsibilities and enabling others to become more responsible.

Employee Choices

Old Tapes	New Approaches
1. **"Guarantee me security."** Tell me the rules and protect me.	There are no guarantees and I have to wake up to the realities facing the organization.
2. **"Be consistent."** Don't tell me one thing today and something else tomorrow.	Tell me the truth, and even if it changes, I will adjust.
3. **"Tell me what to do."** I need direction; give me a recipe.	Let me give you some feedback from my position and let's work out an approach.
4. **"Don't try and make me do your job."** The turf lines are clear; don't cross them.	I recognize that you're under pressure, too. How can we all team up to address the issues we face?

FOUR KEY SKILLS

We have presented the skills and attitudes necessary to cope in a changing environment. They are valid—but unfocused. Or better, there are so many do's and don'ts that it becomes difficult to actually apply them in a consistent manner.

In my work with organizations over the last 10 years I have observed their efforts to cut through all the techniques and formulas available to develop a change strategy. An acquaintance even told me, "I'm not reading or learning anything more. I already know so many things I'm not doing, why bother adding to the list?" As a result of this, I began to try to isolate a core of key skills to deal with change—when it hits and on an ongoing basis. My work extended over a number of years and through a wide variety of organizations. The result was identification of four key skills, from my own experiences, numerous articles and studies, and constant field-testing with my clients. Once they were identified, I worked with International Learning Inc. in Atlanta and with psychologists at Georgia State University to construct and validate a change survey instrument. It is *The Change Readiness Survey*[1]—which I now use in my work.

Our findings reveal that the organizations best equipped to navigate through chaos have established ongoing norms that allow them to (1) foster high communication, (2) provide in-place systems for people support, (3) encourage and reward innovation, risk, and experimentation, and (4) demonstrate corporate and personal openness. Thus, the four key factors are: communication, support, experimentation, and openness.

Communication

Communication will always head the list of organizational needs regardless of whether the environment is changing. The special demand placed on communication in a changing environment, however, is not as a mere function, but rather as an integral strategy in the change process. The communication should also be ongoing and address both intellectual and emotional needs.

Communication is characterized by:

- *Frequency*—Communicates more frequently and less formally; rapid response to events to stay ahead of rumor mill; seeks new and creative means to communicate.
- *Candor*—Communicates both good news and bad news; does not worry about upsetting people; assumes they will be more upset if they are not told.
- *Focus on context*—Assumes that the box has been broken and therefore communicates both tactical (i.e., operational) information and context (i.e., new box) information.
- *Emotional impact*—Recognizes and acknowledges the emotional impact of the information and establishes ongoing means and permission to discuss these issues.

Openness

One of the most important elements in managing change is the ability, on a personal and organizational level, to be open. Organizational openness, presenting thorough and candid information, has already been discussed under communication. Personal openness is an essential factor in creating trust and buy-in. Openness is characterized by:

- *Self-disclosure*—An honest expression of your personal concerns, hopes, thoughts, and worries.

- *Ownership*—Taking an owner's (what are our options?) versus a victim's (they did it to us) point of view, regardless of the circumstances.
- *Reciprocity*—Willingness to listen to and legitimize others' feelings and reactions.

Support

Research shows that one of the most effective strategies to reduce stress, and enable people to begin to move through change, is to allow them to discuss their worries and concerns.[2] Support refers to the establishment of means within the organization allowing people to address their personal feelings and change issues. Support is characterized by:

- *Empathy*—Skills for listening to and demonstrating an understanding of another's point of view or set of feelings.
- *Strategies*—Identifying short-term plans to address personal issues.
- *Establishing norms*—Creating ongoing means for people to express and begin to address their personal issues.

Experimentation

Normative environments claim to value, but generally only pay lip service to, true experimentation, innovation, and risk. Therefore, organizations in a changing environment have a double task: (1) trying to generate new ideas and enable people to try them out, and (2) fighting the entrenched system's reluctance to support experimentation and allow mistakes. Experimentation is characterized by:

- *Legitimizing ideas*—Establishing norms for hearing and fleshing out new ideas and applications.
- *Willingness to experiment*—Encouragement of experimentation and acceptance of mistakes.
- *Seeking input from down the organization*—Willingness to solicit ideas from all levels of the organization and, if necessary, alter established plans created at higher levels in the organization.

CONCLUSION

As you can see, the four skills are not new inventions. Indeed, they are variations of existing, more traditional skills. The only real surprise to me (which it shouldn't have been) was the importance of openness to changing organizations. Its ability to reduce anxiety, focus action, and foster trust is invaluable in those environments.

The four skills themselves function like the four corner stakes of a tent. These stakes are always put in first. They provide the stability and hold the form of the tent. Moreover, they must remain in place both as the tent is going up and when it is being used. If one of these stakes comes out, there's trouble. The remainder of this book will examine these four needs and define the skills associated with them.

Chapter Three

Flipping Your Kayak: Developing Openness

Some people learn from their experiences. Others never recover.

Anonymous

They say that during change, people can get burned out. With me it was closer to cremation. I was telling myself all sorts of terrible things. And what's worse—I believed me.

Person caught in the throes of organizational change

A s a child, I remember watching a TV program about kayakers in a stretch of water the program called the river of no
return. The river, located in South America, literally runs under
a mountain. It enters a cave at one end and comes out at the
other. This fact alone, the narrator mentioned, would dissuade all
but the most courageous. But there was more. The water in the
river was so high that there was not enough room for the kayak
and the kayaker to fit in the cave upright. As a result, on entering
the cave, the kayakers had to flip their kayaks over and ride
upside-down through the pitch-black water, holding their
breaths, until they emerged on the other side.

My cousin and I watched as the kayakers bobbed in clusters at
the entrance of the cave. There they gathered courage and, one
by one, flipped their kayaks and made their runs. I remember
the two of us squirming in discomfort. What if they got stuck?
What if they hit a rock or a log? We stared at the picture of these
people, looking for some clue that would tell where they got
their courage.

FLIPPING YOUR KAYAK

As an adult, I realize that we all have our personal caves to go
through; that getting upended and having to hold our breaths
and come up sputtering is a normal part of life. But is it desirable?
Is it something we look forward to? Generally not.

Most of us, it seems, would rather bob around in the water at
the cave's mouth, safe, upright, and dry, and let somebody else
go through. In a changing environment, however, we might not
have a choice. Many people are on the proverbial river of no return and will be entering the cave whether they like it or not.
These people need to learn how to creatively capsize and how to
hold their breath. In short, they must use the skills that will enable them to enter the cave and come out whole at the other end.

The first step in the process of creative capsizing is what I like
to call looking beneath the waterline. Drawing on the archetypal
symbol for consciousness—water—those things above the waterline are things of which we are aware; those below the line are
things of which we are unaware. The process of making our-

selves aware of those things just below our waterline is the process of developing openness.

As we will discuss in later chapters, openness is a key ingredient in helping us focus outwardly and foster trust in others. In this chapter, however, we want to concentrate on the task of opening ourselves to ourselves. This process is the essential beginning for anyone on the river of no return.

STATED GOALS AND REAL GOALS

To begin this process, think of what you *want* from a change. Wants can be divided into two categories: stated goals and real goals. Here is how they differ:

- Stated goals are what I say I want.
- Real goals are what I really want.

If our stated goals are the same as our real goals, then we feel empowered. If the two differ, then we have problems—we are a house divided. To explain, I offer the story of Rhonda.

The Story of Rhonda

When I was in junior high, we had an annual Spring Dance. One year, I wanted to ask a girl named Rhonda to that dance. Rhonda was tall and slender. She had dark auburn hair and a deep voice, sort of throaty, I remember telling someone. I was hopelessly in love with Rhonda but she scarcely knew I existed. My plan was to call her on the phone. Thus, in the terms of our definition, my stated goal was simply to call Rhonda and invite her to the dance. But now we move to the next question: what was my real goal? There are a variety of possibilities here, but in my case my real goal was not to be rejected. So, the stage is set, and the question becomes: If my stated goal is to ask Rhonda to the dance and my real goal is not to be rejected, are these two goals helping each other or fighting each other? Clearly, they are fighting each other.

The closer I get to achieving my stated goal of asking her, the greater the likelihood that I will be rejected. The next question then becomes: when these two goals are in opposition, what is the effect on my behavior? The simplest answer is tension. In this particular case, it was marked with both extreme tension and ongoing procrastination. I sat in front of the phone marveling at the volume of perspiration two palms could generate. I said finally, "Well, I won't call her tonight. It's too late. I'll talk to her tomorrow in school." The next day, I saw her but was unable to approach. So that night it was back to the phone.

The end of the story is—I never asked Rhonda. Rhonda moved away and I never saw her again. It's clear to me now why I didn't ask Rhonda. At the time, it was not clear. I puzzled: Why aren't I doing what I want to do? If I had gone to a psychologist, the conversation might have gone like this:

Doctor:

Well, Harry, what seems to be the problem?

Harry:

Something's wrong with me. I'm not doing what I want to do.

Doctor:

What did you want to do?

Harry:

Ask Rhonda to the dance.

Doctor:

And you didn't?

Harry:

No.

Doctor:

So, what you're saying is that you wanted to ask Rhonda to the dance. You didn't ask her. As a result you didn't get what you wanted. Right?

Harry:

Exactly.

At this point, the psychologist takes a more kindly approach.

Doctor:

Well, Harry, I've been working with you for a while and I think what you *really* wanted was not to be rejected. By not asking Rhonda you weren't rejected. You got exactly what you wanted.

With his comments the psychologist hopefully expanded my budding adolescent mind. But has he solved my problem? Obviously not. He has, however, given me some information I didn't have. Specifically, he has awakened me to something that was operating in me of which I was unaware. As a result, I now have a choice.

This story points up a key distinction: We are generally aware of our stated goals, but our real goals are often just beneath the level of our awareness—just below the waterline. They include our values, our expectations, our comfort levels, and our fears. They may be working for our best interests or against them. But whatever their effect, we can't see them for what they are, nor can we deal with them, until they have surfaced.

The process of surfacing the things we really want is called insight. When we discover, or someone reminds us, for example, that "what you really seem to want is not to hurt anyone's feelings" or "what you're really after, it seems to me, is a system that will never change." We may respond by saying, "You know, you're right," or "I never thought about it that way, but now that you mention it, I see you have a point." Larry Wilson observes that although we think about a great many things, very often our problem is that "we never think about what we think about." We never reflect on the truth or falsity, the completeness or the incompleteness of our thoughts. The first step in this self-management process, the process of opening up, is for us to "Think about what we think about": to surface some of those real goals that may be getting in our way. To go below the waterline, however, requires that we first flip the kayak.

SELF-INVENTORY

To start this process, it is useful to establish a baseline by responding to seven questions.

1. **What are your concerns or issues regarding a change you are currently experiencing?** This question needs to be viewed broadly. With it, you are throwing out a net. Once answered, it will yield a change event or a series of

events, as well as some specific concerns or issues or reactions you are having.

2. **Is all that true?** This question may or may not be appropriate. Its intent is to soften any overstatements or exaggerations you may have made in question one. Think of it as a checking question.

3. **What do you want from this change?** This is the heart of the process. Respond quickly—from the gut. Given the situation, what do you want?

4. **What do you really want?** Same question, only this time go deeper.

5. **Again, what do you *really* want?** I'm not buying your answers to three and four. What do you really want?

6. **What experience are you looking for?** Net it out. Deep down, given what you really want, what is the experience you're looking for?

7. **What are you willing to give up to get what you want?** You're a realist. You know things don't come free. What are you willing to let go of or do without?

At first glance, these questions seem artificial. For good reason—they are artificial. In their artificiality, however, they are also quite effective, provided you take them seriously. They are the first steps in voluntary capsizing. When I work with groups, I explain the questions much as I have here. I point out that the keys to the process are questions three, four, and five. They are nothing more than asking the same question three times. Most people look at the questions and think, "Well, I know what the answer will be, so I don't see why I have to ask it three times."

They may be surprised when they actually do ask it three times. Taken seriously, the questions act like three strokes of a scalpel, each one going a little deeper. To aid them in this process, I ask them not to work alone but with someone else. They engage in what is known as a "partner interview." Person A uses the seven questions to interview Person B; then they reverse roles. The results are generally both surprising and enlightening. Now I invite you to trust me and do the same. Alone, or with a partner, take 5–10 minutes to respond to the questions and record the answers.

Summing Up

By responding to these questions you have dipped below the waterline enough to catch a glimpse of your real goals. I will refer to this information as we proceed in this section of the book, but I want to briefly address questions three through five. I have found that there are two basic responses to these three questions. Some find that the answers remain basically the same, but become much more specific. The majority find that the answers change and become more personal as they move from three to five. The following is a sample of typical reactions:

> It was really interesting to have to answer the same question three times. I had to really think and go deeper each time.
>
> I thought the answers would be the same. But they weren't.
>
> The answers at first were sort of standard. But as I went through it, they got more personal.
>
> I didn't like what I ended up with. But it was *true*.
>
> The answer I got for question 5 seemed sort of selfish, almost egotistical.

To gain a sense of the changes between questions three and five, compare the following:

Typical responses to question three:

- Be an effective manager,
- Keep my job.
- Hold my unit together.
- Develop a new marketing plan.
- Make myself marketable outside the organization.

Typical responses to question five:

- Gain the recognition I deserve.
- Avoid a confrontation with the organization.
- Maintain my current status.
- Avoid hurting anyone's feelings.
- Make the right choice.

As you can see, the latter group is more personal and sounds a little egotistical. It is important to remember, however, that the purpose of asking the questions is not to come up with necessarily positive answers. Rather it is to come up with the truth—to come up with your real goals. In general, answers to the third question tend to be standard, acceptable, or organizational responses. Responses to the fourth and fifth questions, however, tend to be more personal and real. In short, whether you like them or not, they give you an idea of what is really motivating you. To examine the effects of these real goals on a person's ability to successfully cope with change, we need to look at a series of case studies.

CASE STUDIES IN CHANGE

Robert

Robert is a senior manager in a Fortune 100 high-tech computer firm. Because of competition and constantly shifting markets, Robert's firm has decided to take an unprecedented step and go into competition with its own customers. His firm will continue their bread and butter business of selling computer components to companies that manufacture mainframes, but they will also start to make mainframes themselves.

At first the company's sales force was shocked by this move. Even before the company manufactured a single mainframe, the rumor of their strategy had caused tension between the sales force and long-time customers who felt betrayed. To both the sales force and the client firms this strategy seemed self-defeating. To develop a mainframe business, in which they were unproven, at the cost of a highly successful component business and good will among long-time customers didn't seem to make sense.

Not so, says the company—and they want Robert to deliver that message. The mainframe market is large and getting larger, with plenty of room for everybody. The perception of double-dealing, however, is a problem—and it is Robert's problem. He has to not only sell the idea to prospective mainframe customers but also justify the strategy to the company's existing customers, and furthermore, explain the new strategy to his company's sales force. "So, what am I?" Robert asks. "A marketer, a customer relations person, or an employee relations manager?" "All of the above," the company responds. Robert's job is complex and challenging. His new job calls for creativity and bold action.

Thus, Robert's stated goal is nothing less than to formulate and sell the company's new marketing strategy—and the company's future. So far, Robert is not getting the results for which he or the company had hoped. His ideas and his new strategies, although sound and well planned, seem to be falling just short of what is needed. What neither Robert nor the company knows is that Robert's real goal is getting in his way.

Laura

Laura is the section supervisor in a large medical facility. One year ago, Laura would have said she was the nursing supervisor in a large hospital, but since that time her hospital and another hospital and a large clinic merged to become one corporate identity. The employees of all three institutions tend to avoid words such as merger, corporation, and new management because they make the new entity sound too corporate, a word that has a negative connotation. "We're in health care, after all, not in business."

"Not so," says the new breed of health care managers proliferating through the new entity, "we are in business, whether we like to admit it or not." What with rising medical costs, HMOs, competition for hospital beds and medical services, and new government regulations for health care funding, we need to become more and more businesslike. It's a matter of survival."

"But at what cost?" the medical staff counters. "What about our commitment to quality and patient care?" For some reason, there is a perception that business and quality care are inversely related, that the more systematic and efficient the facility becomes, the more impersonal and uncaring its treatment of patients becomes. At least that's what Laura fears. When she asks, "What is the scope of my new job?" Her hospital administrator tells her, half facetiously, half seriously, "Well, Laura, we were hoping you could tell us."

Her primary task now, as the hospital administrator alluded, is to redefine her own job so she can function in a wider network. In general, she is finding that she needs to be more of an influencer than a controller; she needs to coordinate teams more than direct a staff. As someone who had traditionally run a fairly tight ship, the idea of giving away power and relying on others to implement policies over which she had control is difficult.

Laura's stated goal is to ensure the smooth functioning of people and departments in three formerly separate institutions while maintaining the responsiveness and quality care for which her unit is known. At a deeper level, however, she has a real goal working at cross-purposes to her intentions.

Steve

Steve works in the data processing department of a large bank. His bank recently acquired several smaller banks, and Steve has been moved from one position to another to help coordinate their different data processing systems. Steve doesn't mind being moved around and he is a good troubleshooter. He is competent and has creative ideas for merging systems. People trust his expertise and rely on his judgment. Even the rumors now afoot that their bank might be acquired don't really bother him. He is capable, willing to relocate, and enjoys his work.

Recently, his bank has been considering a complete switchover from one computer system to another. One of the banks they acquired, although much smaller, had a very smooth-running and efficient operations function. At first, it was thought that this system, despite its advantages, would be inappropriate for the larger bank network, but now they are reconsidering. The cost of switching over would be great, but with some minor adjustments and expansions, the new system could, in the long run, serve the bank much better than the present system.

"Not so," says Steve. Elegant though it may be, he contends, it does not have the flexibility needed to handle the growth the bank is likely to experience in the next 5 to 10 years. Others disagree and think the present system will be outmoded in 5 to 10 years. The decision has pretty much been made that they will go to the new system. They are counting on Steve to help make that happen. His response is, "I wouldn't have made that decision. But as long as that's the way it's going to be, I'll do everything I can to make it work." Steve's stated goal is to make the new system succeed. What he doesn't know is that he is about to run headlong into his real goal.

Marilyn

Marilyn has been a school principal for eight years. During that time, and particularly during the 25 years she has been in education, she has seen a lot of change. At one point, with more than 15 years of experience, she was almost laid off due to shrinking enrollments. She survived. Marilyn has been through a great deal and until a year ago was looking forward to stability and peace of mind. "Not so," said the district.

The movement away from neighborhood schools to larger school conglomerates and magnet schools hit home. Her district was merged with another district. Marilyn kept her job, or rather she kept her position. Her job however, changed dramatically. She was put in charge of closing her current building, relocating, and merging her staff with another staff in a new and very large building. At first, this news was a bombshell, but Marilyn's positive attitude and ability with people served her well. She also had the sense to delegate the details—usually her weak suit—to her assistant principal and give him complete freedom and authority to work them out.

It turned out fairly well. They mourned the loss of their older, more familiar setting and were particularly sad about the loss of some teachers to transfers and layoffs. But, in general, Marilyn's sensitivity to both the faculty and the parents allowed her to make the best of the situation. Although people may not have been altogether happy with the outcome, they at least trusted Marilyn and thought she was doing the best job she could under the circumstances.

Marilyn's stated goal is to form intact work teams to plan and implement a series of new programs, some of them very exciting. For reasons Marilyn can't put her finger on, however, it's not going as well as she or the faculty would like. The problem—Marilyn's real goal—is still beneath the waterline.

FIVE FATAL FEARS

There are as many real goals as there are people. For our purposes here, and in order to unravel the obstacles that Robert, Laura, Steve, and Marilyn are running into, we are going to concentrate on five.[1] They are: the need to succeed, to be right, to be loved, to be in control, and to be comfortable.

To succeed	The desire to succeed in my job, my relationships, or my life; to be seen as successful; to be rewarded accordingly; to receive the esteem reserved for successful persons.
To be right	The desire to be correct, accurate, or thorough; to work from information and data rather than from intuition; to be able to select the right choice from alternatives; to have assurances and guarantees.
To be loved	The desire to have people think well of me, to like me, or to love me; to not offend people or hurt their feelings; to foster harmonious working relationships and teamwork; to make people happy.
To be in control	The desire to know and be able to regulate all the variables; to not be left in the dark or be on the receiving end of surprises; to be in charge and to direct efforts according to a plan; to be able to predict accurately.
To be comfortable	The desire to retain peace of mind and not experience stress; to avoid emotional or physical pain; to be able to use energy to be creative and productive rather than have to confront difficulties or solve problems.

In their own right, there is nothing necessarily wrong with wanting to succeed, to be right, to be loved, to be in control, and to be comfortable. As most people realize, they cannot be all of these things all of the time. If they were to think about it, they would probably find that during the most productive periods in their life they were out of control and very uncomfortable. If not taken to extremes, the five basic wants listed are legitimate goals. The problem arises when these goals are not nice-to-haves but must-haves. These goals, as nice-to-haves, give us a sense of equilibrium and can function as barometers by telling us when to exert a little more effort. But as must-haves, these goals become tyrannical, emotional taskmasters, demanding that we must succeed, must be right, must be loved, must be in control, and must be comfortable—or else.

Or else what? "Or else it will be terrible and I will not be able to tolerate it and I will have to do all in my power to stop it! Fix it! Bring it back to where and what it ought to be!"

This line of logic is not exaggerated. We can see it happening to a lesser or greater degree almost every day. Usually we see it in others before we see it in ourselves; and we tend to see it when there has been some disruption of the norms—in other words, in times of change. Consider the man whose opinion, when confronted, suddenly becomes an immutable law of nature. "Now this is the way it is!" he states, and will entertain no contending opinion. Later, on reflection, he realizes that his opinion was not the only way, and wonders why he had such a need to be right. Or the woman who, when things don't go quite as planned, suddenly takes over, declaring, "OK. Enough of this fooling around. We aren't getting anywhere. So Tom, you do this, and Sally, you do that. Now!" Later, looking back on the episode, the woman wonders why it was so important to railroad people and subject them to her need to be in control.

The reasons why we suddenly revert to these singular behaviors are beyond the scope of this discussion. Suffice it to say that (1) they exist, and (2) they are apt to flare up during times of change and transition. When they do flare up, they block our ability to think and act and relate. They suddenly become the most important things in our lives and they control our behavior. The reasons for their power has to do with fear.

Think of it this way. The desire to be in control, for example, results in activities such as getting a little more organized, or clarifying some roles. If I feel I absolutely *need* to control, however, then I generate a fear of being out of control, which is then likely to generate a much stronger set of behaviors to make darn sure I'm in control—whether anybody likes it or not. Thus, a need tends to generate a corresponding fear.

The Need to	Generates Fear of
Succeed	Failure
Be right	Mistakes (or being wrong)
Be loved	Rejection
Be in control	Surprises
Be comfortable	Pain

Before using this information to look more closely at Robert, Laura, Steve, and Marilyn, it is important to address two questions: Is this information true? Is this information useful?

Is this information true? No. The inner motivations and real goals of people do not fall neatly into five categories. On the other hand, a great many of our inner motivations and real goals can be described in terms of these five categories. The list has validity in that people can generally see in themselves some of the fears listed, and in so doing have begun recognizing things about themselves that were previously below the waterline.

Is this useful? Yes. It is useful to the extent that it states a process of recognizing and confronting attitudes which may be having an effect, a negative effect, of which we may be only dimly aware. It also provides a model and some language. We may be able to substitute words such as need to win rather than to succeed, or fear of being left out rather than fear of rejection. In any case, the model and its language are meant to be descriptive rather than prescriptive. It succeeds not when it is telling you what you are, but rather when it enables you to describe yourself. In this spirit we can examine the circumstances of our four people.

Robert

Robert's stated goal is to formulate and sell his company's new marketing strategy. More than that, however, he also has to come up with ways to sell the idea to existing customers (who see it as a conflict of interest) and ways to sell it within the organization. Robert finds himself in a common situation for the present era of change. His past skills and accomplishments qualify him for only part of the task he must address. To accomplish this task will involve creativity and a certain amount of courage, attributes which Robert has demonstrated in the past.

That is his problem. Early in his career, when the company was still forming and he had nothing to lose, Robert was creative and bold. He succeeded and continued to succeed. Robert had surely read or heard that "nothing fails like success." He was undoubtedly familiar with the Peter Principle asserting that "people tend to rise to their level of incompetence." Whether he applied them to himself in any real way is hard to say, but in my conversations with him, one thing became clear: He had developed a fear, as he puts it, of blowing it. Robert developed a fear of failure bred of a need to succeed.

The results were easy to see. In his work, he applied the old saying—if all you have is a hammer, everything looks like a nail. He applied traditional marketing techniques to all three areas of his task when these techniques were appropriate to only one of them. Moreover, he has consistently been reluctant to incorporate anything bold or creative, even though he has had ideas along those lines. Robert's stated goal of developing a strategy is being hamstrung by his real goal: the need to succeed, and its attendant fear of failure. Robert won't take chances; he refuses to implement or even propose anything that isn't assured of success.

Postscript. Robert has not been able to flip his kayak, hold his breath, and go through the cave of risk. His real goal is still beneath the level of his awareness—masquerading as prudent caution, smart planning, and guaranteed results. At last report he was shifted to focusing exclusively on marketing efforts. The potential personal benefits to Robert never came to pass and the company is still wrestling with the misunderstandings of their clients and sales force.

You don't have to be a manager in a high-tech company to understand Robert's situation. There are many like him, people whose sense that they need to succeed and must not fail prevents them from recognizing, much less actually trying, something new. Ironically, the need and opportunities for risky creative action have seldom been greater. True, organizations do not help the matter when they demand normative results and assurances in a changing environment. But in the final analysis, I have found that real goals—in this case, a need to succeed—are the hidden root causes of the shortcoming of the larger corporate attitudes.

Laura

Laura's stated goal was to ensure the smooth functioning of people in three formerly separate institutions who are now employees of the same institution, while maintaining their reputation for responsiveness and quality care. Initially, Laura saw this challenge as playing to her strong suit: control. Who better, the administration thought, to head up this challenging task than a proven entity like Laura?

Like Robert, Laura tried to tackle her new job by applying old rules. She set up a structured system in which she could direct the new entity and maintain quality. Unlike Robert, Laura found out very quickly that her systems were not going to work. She was able to maintain an acceptable level of quality care, but at great cost. The unit was overworked and highly stressed. When the patients began to sense that something was wrong, Laura knew that something would have to be done. To assure continued quality, she would have to give up control. This realization was frightening and she told me it broke over her in three stages. The first was complete devastation and fear. It did not start as a logical and pristine phrase, such as "I need to relinquish control." Rather it came as, "I'm incompetent. I can't handle this job." The second stage was a glimmer of what the needed new skills might be. While she had been trying, and failing, to control the new systems, the employees had been improvising ideas behind her back simply to maintain their level of care. Noticing this, it occurred to Laura that maybe that was the solution. The third phase was a mixture of depression and relief: depression that she was not up to the task, relief knowing she could ask for help.

Laura kept all these emotions hidden. Her feelings of worthlessness, fear, hope, depression, and relief, real though they were, seldom broke the surface. In that regard, Laura is like many of us who are going through change. We are beset with a series of reactions that are often quite new to us. Many of these feelings are unfounded and pass quickly, but others are not. They hang on and sap our energy and our ability to respond.

Postscript. Laura came out fine. Interestingly, her need to control was less personal than it was professional. Her high control needs were more the result of an artificial sense of professionalism (how supervisors act) and duty (what quality care ought to be). Once she saw that neither pose was necessary, she was able to drop the posing. Specifically, once she saw that others could function just fine on their own (with minimal supervision) and still maintain care levels, she let them go. Looking back, Laura feels lucky. She feels that she would have been indefinitely condemned to an internal war of emotions if it were not for the fact that the situation made her change. Employee tension and the threat of a decline in quality forcibly flipped her kayak and circumstances held her head underwater until she opened her eyes.

Steve

Steve's stated goal was quite simple: to make the new computer system succeed. It is not the system he would have chosen; not the one he thinks is best. But having gone on record, he settled in to make it work.

During the initial stages in the changeover from one system to another, Steve pointed out some key shortcomings of the new system. It wasn't surprising—everybody knew the new system would have holes. Under Steve's careful scrutiny, however, these holes were plugged and the system was able to function. Over time, this pattern began to repeat itself: system falters, Steve fixes; system falters, Steve fixes. Steve's ability to cope with the continual changes was nothing short of heroic.

That's when the trouble started. The flow of ideas and suggestions from other people in the computer area began to run into roadblocks. "No, that won't work," Steve told one person. "Maybe, but it doesn't fit with the plan," he told another. "We can't take the risk," he told a third. "What risk?" the person asked. "The risk of going down a blind alley. This thing's gotta be right," Steve said. And Steve was sure it was right, just like all, or most, of his other ideas. Without realizing it, Steve had fallen into a normative mindset (I've gotten the pattern) while he was still in a formative or exploratory mode. Drawing on the strength of his abilities, he had established a track record of making good decisions, of being right. Banking that he could sustain that track record, he developed a plan that allowed for no mistakes. Consequently, his mindset changed from solving problems to avoiding mistakes. Finally, however, the system was simply not performing to the needed level. Steve's need to be right and his fear of mistakes was taking an ever mounting toll, in terms of efficiency and of human relationships. The sharp edge of his superior ability was now cutting the other way. Finally, in the midst of trying to justify himself one day, his boss cut him off mid-sentence with: "Steve, people either get results or they give reasons. Which are you?"

Postscript. Sobered by his boss's challenge, Steve was able to let go a little and allow the system to find its way to handle the load. But for Steve, there is still a nagging sense that if they had given his plan a little more time, it would have worked. On the other side of his emotional coin is a lingering feeling of shame that he was wrong. Both attitudes, direct results of his strong need to be right and his fear of mistakes, continue to preoccupy him and detract from his ability to work productively and creatively. When I last talked to him, he was slipping more and more into cynicism and a sense of having been set up.

Marilyn

Marilyn's stated goal was to form intact work teams to plan and implement a series of new programs in her magnet school. She started by asking people what they wanted to do and what the teams should look like. She planned to let her assistant principal do the actual administrative work while she would float, offering support to teams and to individuals. Everything started off just fine. Soon, however, Marilyn found herself getting involved in the mechanics of team assignments. "See Bob," she would say. "That's his job."

"That's the problem," they would counter. "Bob doesn't understand what we're trying to do." Marilyn spoke to Bob about the problem. Drawing on his experience as a history teacher, he quoted one line from the lore of World War I: "Entangling Alliances." The teachers came from different schools with different programs. They had a strong sense of with whom they could work and with whom they couldn't. "You're going to have to make some hard decisions about who's going to do what and who's going to be with whom," he told Marilyn. Instantly, she felt a twinge run through her. "No," she said, "They have to work it out themselves."

"Well, you tell them then," Bob said. "They won't listen to me." Marilyn didn't want to summarily dictate teams. She wanted her people to work it out. She didn't want to pressure any individuals. She didn't want any dissension. She wanted a cooperative, collaborative team. At least that's what she told herself. But what she really wanted was to be liked, respected, and accepted. She was afraid of being rejected.

This fear of not being loved caused Marilyn to avoid making decisions lest she hurt anybody's feelings. The last thing she wanted, she told herself, was to force people to do something they didn't want to do. Ironically, by trying not to make people mad at her, she made everybody mad at her.

Postscript. Marilyn's school seems to be functioning well now. Programs are up and running and the teachers are in teams. Not everybody is happy, but they're mostly getting over it. The teachers still admire Marilyn—but more as a martyr than an able administrator. Rather than take sides or take any real action, she chose to cajole and coax until everybody ended up on a team and Marilyn ended up with large bags under her eyes.

This need to be liked is one of the most common real goals I run into in various organizations. In the changing environments, things are tense already. So the last thing anybody wants is to ruffle anybody's feathers any more. The result is simply avoiding or putting off doing the right things for fear of hurting people's feelings and becoming unpopular.

SELF-INVENTORY REVISITED

Now that you have had the opportunity to see real goals at work in people's lives, you may want to take a second look at the self-inventory questions that were introduced earlier. You may have answered them conscientiously at that time, but more likely you breezed by. In any case, I want to give you another opportunity to ask yourselves these questions—or better, ask someone else to ask you these questions. As mentioned, when another person interviews you, using these questions, there is a tendency for more complete and honest answers. The whole process takes 10 minutes or less. It is time well spent. For your convenience, the questions have been repeated in this section. Remember, this is a structured interview. It is also a tool; something that can be used on an ongoing basis to help you stop and examine your reactions to change. It may seem somewhat artificial at first. But, as you get into it, it enables you, in an efficient way, to begin the process of uncovering your real goals.

STRATEGIES FOR SELF-MANAGEMENT

Thus far we have distinguished real goals from stated goals and provided some examples of each. The self-inventory is a tool designed to help you begin to make those distinctions for yourself. Once you have done that you can move to the next step: self-management.

Self-management is a widely used term with a number of definitions. For our purposes here I want to define it simply as:

1. Aligning stated and real goals.
2. Focusing on realistic action steps.

Think of it in terms of energy conservation. I like to think that when I get up in the morning that I have a full tank of gas—call it 100 units of energy—to use any way I want. I use one unit to

Self-Inventory

1. What are your concerns or issues regarding a change you are currently experiencing?

2. Is all that true?

3. What do you want from this change?

4. What do you really want?

5. Again, what do you really want?

6. What experience are you looking for?

7. What are you willing to give up to get what you want?

shave and brush my teeth, two units to get dressed and get going, etc. Then, depending on the day, I head off to work, go on an outing with my family, mow the lawn, or any number of other things. If, in that activity, what I say I want and what I really want are the same, I am productive, using my energy very efficiently. But if the two are opposed, then suddenly there is a huge energy drain. The conflict in me devours my dwindling energy units at an alarming rate. In order for me to return to a state of efficient energy use (and decreased tension), I must first somehow align what I say I want and what I really want so that they are the same.

For example, if my stated goal is to mend fences with someone whom I have offended, but my real goal is to get even, then my apology will probably sound hollow. To align these two opposed goals, I can change my stated goal to getting even, or change my real goal to mending fences. (I hope I would select the latter.) But the basic principle is clear: When the two goals are opposed, one of them needs to be changed to match the other.

The process of discovering the exact identity of the real goal is, as we have seen, a demanding process requiring courage and discernment. It appears to be easier when someone else is present to bounce things off of. Counselors make a living helping people in this process.

The process of surfacing submerged issues and taking action need not be a complicated process. Christine's experience illustrates this process.

Christine

Christine works in the marketing department of a large firm. Her firm was recently acquired by an even larger firm and the two marketing functions were merged. When the reorganization was announced, Christine was not happy. She found herself in a position lower than that of certain people who didn't have as much experience as she did. They had more credentials, but they were, in Christine's opinion, not as savvy and certainly not as knowledgeable as she.

When Christine asked herself what, in effect, is question three, "What do you want?" She answered quickly: "To be in charge of one of the teams." She felt she had earned it. The resulting discussion between Christine and her new boss became hopelessly deadlocked as Christine argued the greater value of her direct experience over that of credentials and of the indirect experience of some of the other team members. At the end of the discussion, Christine felt devalued and vowed to look for work elsewhere.

At this point, depressed and angry, Christine decided to flip her kayak and went through the questioning process in earnest.

What do you really want?

"I want to be recognized for my contributions and not seen as someone with limited abilities and therefore a junior member of the team."

"*Are* your abilities limited? I asked.

"Well," she said. "Maybe." This answer uncovered a new level and she went to the next question.

Try again, what do you *really* want?

Her answers came quickly. "To be respected. To expand my experience base. To be a valued fully functioning member of the team."

With these three real goals, she was able to examine certain assumptions implicit in these statements:

1. Respect. Was it true that she was not respected? She decided that it was true. Certain other team members did not include Christine in their marketing clique because she hadn't had the experience they had. The fact she had done well in the old firm carried little weight with them. She was afraid they didn't really take her seriously.

2. Experience. Why did she want to expand her experience base? The answer was simple. Her experience was limited. She knew a lot about a little, and her insistence that her experience qualified her as an equal only caused others to question her experience—and also not take her seriously.

3. Team. She felt she was not valued as a functioning member. But, she asked herself, how much of that was the superior attitude of other team members and how much was caused by her

demand to be in charge of a team? She decided it was a little of both. Adding all of these factors together, Christine revised what she felt addressed the sum-up question:

What experience are you looking for?

> To be a valued team member, respected for my specific contributions; and to be given opportunities to expand my experience base with an eye on eventually heading up a team.

Christine's is now a more realistic real goal. In terms of the five needs discussed earlier, we can see elements of wanting to be loved, wanting to succeed, and perhaps wanting to be in control. Any extended comparisons along these lines, however, are purely academic. The primary point is that Christine has looked beneath the surface, and under the stated goal of heading a team—which was, in reality, a narrow and tyrannical emotional demand—were the real goals and the experience of respect, acceptance, and growth. Also, because she has faced squarely her strengths as well as her limitations, the real goals will help her define a direction and take action rather than generate fear.

Finally, what is Christine willing to give up? She found she was willing, if not to give up, at least to postpone being a team leader. She is also willing to give up some of her time to expand her experience base.

Do these revelations solve Christine's problem? No. When she comes up sputtering at the other end of the cave she may find that she is butting up against a good-old-boy network and will always be seen as a gofer. In which case she should probably leave. On the other hand, her expanded sense of herself may allow her to grow and move up in the system. Whatever the outcome, Christine has a more realistic sense of what she really wants and therefore a greater sense of control over her direction. She is no longer a house divided, working at cross-purposes to herself.

CONCLUSION

The main points of this chapter are:

- Stated and real goals are quasi-psychological terms which are useful in making a basic distinction between our intentions (what we say we want) and our heart's desires (what we really want).

- We are usually aware of our stated goals. They exist in the form of promises we make to ourselves, job duties, assignments from the boss, New Year's resolutions, things we read in books, etc.
- We are generally not as aware of our real goals as we are of our stated goals, but these real goals have their effect on us nevertheless.
- Real goals exist at a variety of levels within us. Our purpose here is to identify those that may be affecting our attitudes toward change. To address the more deeply seated issues requires the skills of professional psychologists and counselors.
- Once we begin to surface some of our own real goals, we become more open and are in a better position to take action to deal with change.

The technique—the openness skill—that will help you actually apply this information is the set of seven Self-Inventory questions. At first, this may seem too simplistic for such a weighty topic. Indeed, there are more complex and involved tools for self-management. But for the purposes of being able to stop and check one's own stated and real goals this technique is both valuable and easy to do.

I don't recommend doing it every day when you get up in the morning. It is meant to be used when you experience tension, worry, a sense of unsureness, a challenge, anger, a strong need to act—these are the reactions common to people in change telling them that there may be a difference between their stated and real goals. The technique has the effect of being able to remove blinders and create options. In Christine's case, for example, she was able to move through the demand to be a team leader to a realization that the experience she was looking for had more to do with respect and growth. This is not to say that Christine would not have made a good team leader. She may have. But given the realities and the politics, she was able to give herself more room in which to operate. But it took a conscientious answering of the questions to get her there. The key is discipline.

I can't force you to take the inventory in a book format. In my workshops, however, I almost always have people engage in a partner interview, using these questions. The results are always the same. They look at me funny at first, but then afterwards the exercise always has among the highest, or the highest rating.

The technique is deceptively simple. But the repeated, "What do you want?" questions have a nagging, demanding quality that force people to cut through the externals to the core. Then, the "What experience are you looking for?" helps you reframe your real goal. This process plus the construct of the five fatal fears can then lead to insights on which you can act. It takes discipline, but it works.

The bottom-line benefit of this process finally can be best understood in terms of fear and anxiety. The difference between fear and anxiety is that fear has an object whereas anxiety has no object. Given a choice between fear and anxiety most people choose fear because they know what they are up against and can take action. The effect of the proposed technique is to help you translate your anxiety into fear. "You came here anxious," I explain to my audiences, "and I want to send you away fearful." They laugh (most of the time) but theirs is a laughter of recognition. They know that managing change is not like taking a pill. It is a passage, not an event.

The intent of this chapter is to make the beginnings of that passage more focused. And it has also offered the assurance that the cave does end and that by cultivating a greater sense of openness you will be able to right your kayak, sputtering but more empowered, on the other side.

Chapter Four

Beyond Mark Twain: Communicating Change

They told us the change would be like the flicker of a lightbulb. They were wrong. It was a total blackout.

Employee in a changing organization

The employees watch me carefully. They take their cues from my behavior. If I'm not open and honest, I've lost 'em.

Manager in a changing organization

S amuel Langhorne Clemens got his pen name, Mark Twain, from his experience as a riverboat pilot on the Mississippi. Mississippi riverboats routinely stationed one person at the bow to throw a line with a weight on its end into the water to test for depth. "Mark Twain" for two fathoms was the all-clear signal: the water was deep enough to allow the boat to pass. Although navigating the Mississippi was dangerous and took a great deal of skill—and not a few boats sunk or went aground—it was still basically a normative activity. The combination of accurate maps and a finite set of navigating skills made travel on the river relatively safe. Thus the cadences of the man on the bow, calling out the depth readings, was the major form of communication and feedback to the pilot. He communicated confirmations or exceptions to an otherwise known system.

In a white-water environment, such a one-dimensional and leisurely system would be useless. The chaos of a raging river requires a vastly more complex and rapid information and feedback system. Why is it then that organizations and people still rely on their standard information systems in a changing environment? The answer is simply habit, and also cost—cost of money, time, and effort. In a changing environment, however, organizations need to think carefully about how and what to communicate. Otherwise, the information runs ahead of them, out of control and inaccurate, via the rumor mill.

Also, changing environments bring in a factor other than the need for information, namely the need for trust. Because of its incompleteness, because of its volatility, and because of its changeability, information in a changing environment cannot be trusted, that is, trusted in the way normative information can be trusted. So if I can't trust the information, then I had better be able to trust the person providing it. As a result, the element of trust and its vehicle—openness—becomes as important as the information, perhaps more so. In either case, an effective communication process is one of the most essential skills for navigating in chaos. It is a key aspect of managing change not to leave it to memos, to the untrained, or to chance.

The Hollywood image of the depth tester on Mark Twain's riverboat was always that of a leisurely, semi-involved, low-level functionary, often a young boy. Similarly, organizations have traditionally relegated communication to a mere function; and even when, in crisis, the CEO attempts to deliver the information, the result is often rote or self-serving. The image of the communicator in a changing environment needs to be one of an aware and sensitive deliverer who has thought through the implications and impact of the message and is intellectually and emotionally prepared to deliver it.

In Chapter 2, we identified four key factors that need to be addressed in changing environments: communication, openness, support, and experimentation. In Chapter 3, we presented insights and skills for developing openness. In this chapter we are going to continue our discussion of openness and link it with communication. We address them together because they are integrally related under the heading of what I call transparency skills. When organizations or people are closed or opaque, they are inaccessible. They repel approaches and foster distrust. But when people and organizations are transparent, then we can see into them; we know what to expect and we feel more in control. The purpose of this chapter is to lay out some basic communication principles for a changing environment and present a single skill, a template that can be adapted effectively in a variety of change situations.

THREE MEETINGS

The vice president approached the podium, paused and drew a deep breath, seemingly to gather his courage and composure. The employees waited anxiously for his message. They had all just been through a sudden and far-reaching reorganization. They had lost some people and there were rumors more would be cut. The vice president opened with a faint "Good afternoon." There was a tone of weariness in his voice. "This last week has been rough—probably the roughest I've ever seen." He went on to briefly summarize the events of the week and very candidly expressed his own feelings about those events. He used phrases like "I'm worried about that, I'm hopeful in this area, I think this was a mistake and I'm going to bat for us to try and right it," and "I think this is probably a good idea, but I'm not sure." He then went on to thank the people for their efforts to cope, outlined a few tentative steps they were planning to take and promised to keep them informed.

It was a good meeting. Nothing was solved. Indeed, the situation threatened to get worse before it got better. But still it was a good meeting because of two key factors: The executive told the truth and he let people know how he was feeling. People felt that they got honest information—not as much as they would have liked, and certainly not what they would call good news—but honest information nevertheless. They appreciated that and they also felt they could trust him. He delivered the message from the heart, and that was worth something. I had the sense at the time that this meeting went very well, but I couldn't put my finger on exactly why. Later, after other meetings, the reasons became clearer.

The organization did a fairly good job of keeping people informed and in about a month the vice president called a second meeting. He said he was feeling better but not great. He said he could see progress and briefly summarized some of his reasons. He thanked the people for their efforts. This meeting, too, was successful. The sense of honesty and trust continued.

Then came the third meeting. The vice president approached the lectern with a quickness in his step that hadn't been there before. "I'm feeling great," he announced. "It's been a rough two months, but I think we're finally coming out of it." He went on to cite facts that indicated some improvement, but surely did not merit the kind of optimism he projected. Then he apologized for having been a sad sack in the previous meetings. He said he was counting on them to "take the bull by the horns and start to thrive on chaos because there was certainly plenty of it going around."

There was an uncomfortable silence in the room. Finally, one man, Frank, raised his hand and said in a very honest way that he was glad some people were feeling positive but that in his area there were still problems and people were still struggling and certainly not even close to hopeful yet. The vice president picked up on Frank's tone and in an empathic manner said, "Well, Frank . . . thanks for being frank." There was a murmur of laughter. He then made a statement that to the best of my recollection went something like: "And if you feel that way, I don't know, maybe the best thing is—well, maybe this isn't the company for you."

A gasp shot through the room. I don't think the vice president meant his statement the way it came out, but it was too late. The audience had heard, "love it or leave it." He began a nervous attempt to explain his way out of the dilemma but wisely chose to shut up. Then, after a moment's pause he again thanked Frank for his honesty, looked up and asked cheerfully, "Anybody else here feel like Frank?" Dead silence.

What had happened? Clearly the vice president put his foot in his mouth. But there is more to it than just that. That meeting was in trouble long before Frank raised his hand. And what had gone right in the first meetings to make them come off so well? There are some obvious answers and some not so obvious. To answer these questions, we need to look at change in terms of "N."

THE "N" DIAGRAM

"N" represents where an organization is at any point in time. Thus "N" can stand for now, normal, or neutral. Or perhaps for no good or never again. Whatever you select, point N is your present state. Organizations in change tend to see themselves as moving from N forward—to plus one.

Plus one represents progress. It represents improvement on the present state. If we are too large at N, plus one is downsizing; if we're too small, plus one is expansion. Common plus-one scenarios include:

- We're too internally focused. We've got to shift from a production to a marketing mentality.

- We've taken our success for granted. We've got to become more innovative.
- We've lost sight of what our customers really want. We've got to improve our customer service.
- We're too provincial. We've got to take a global point of view.

In short, plus-one logic says that we've got to do something to handle the chaos we've got or we've got to create some chaos of our own.

In virtually all the organizations with whom I have consulted, I've never known anyone to disagree with the logic of plus one. On the contrary, they accept it readily, saying such things as, "It's long overdue," or "We don't have a choice. It's a survival issue," or "It's about time. We need a little new blood." N plus one, then, is a valid way to describe the organization's intellectual/technical response to change. But now, how about the employees, supervisors, managers—and their families—how do they respond?

No matter how positive a change may be; no matter how necessary or essential, individual people—human beings—tend to respond to change initially at least, not by jumping forward to plus one, but by in effect being knocked *back* a square—to minus one. The key word at minus one is loss. When change hits, people feel that they have either lost something or stand to lose something.

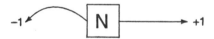

I talk to a lot of groups about change. When I present the plus one side of this model, I have their polite attention. But they've heard it before. They agree, but also feel mildly uncomfortable, waiting for the inevitable inspirational speech exhorting them to get in there and embrace change! But when I draw the arrow backward to minus one, and particularly when I lay out the four-letter word loss, they change. Eyes open, backs straighten, heads nod. I have hit their real issue. At that point I can stop my formal presentation and simply ask: What are the losses people feel at minus one? They usually fall out very quickly as follows:

Security:

"Will I have a job? And if I do, what will it be?"

Security issues range from job security to more general and non-specific concerns about the loss of an environment that was known and comfortable.

Control:

"Who will be in charge? What will be expected of me?"

Control issues usually center around systems and procedures. People are often rewarded according to how well they "control" their responsibilities. To alter the control structure threatens the loss of a person's ability to achieve.

People:

"What about our team? We were a *family*. What will happen to us?"

People or affiliation concerns often top the list of employee concerns. Teams, groups working together for years, are highly valued. To break them up results in losses of relationships and also potential losses of efficiency.

Competence:

"I was good at what I did . . . and now look what you've done to me!"

Competency equals mastery. So, when you change somebody's job—even if it's a better job, a promotion, with more money and responsibility—the person becomes, technically speaking, incompetent to a certain degree. Outwardly, the person acknowledges the opportunity and necessity of learning new skills. But inwardly, he or she may be thinking: What if I can't make it? What if I've finally reached the level of my incompetence?

Identity, or future:

"I used to work for Pat, but now what am I?"

Where is my career going? People often pin their identity, their careers and therefore their future on where and for whom they work. To alter these basic facts results in a perceived loss of identity and a sense of being cut loose to drift.

Are these perceived losses true? Will the dreaded consequences of the change really come to pass? The answer is: Sometimes, yes; generally, no. The truth or falsity of the fears is not as important an issue, however, as the effect of the fears on the individuals' and organizations' ability to cope.

I often ask groups, "If you're at minus one, concerned about your losing control, becoming incompetent, losing your friends, and wondering who you are, and the company comes at you from plus one saying, 'Change is great! You really ought to want it,' what's your response? How do you feel?"

The answers?

"Lousy." "That's your agenda." "Talk to someone who cares."

In answer to these negative reactions, organizations often respond with incredulity. "I don't understand you. These plus one changes are so necessary, so positive, that anyone who's having a problem must either be stupid or have a bad attitude. In their haste to deal with their own problems and get onto solutions as quickly as possible, organizations tend to ignore—or view as an inconvenience—the reactions of the people *in* those organizations. They are saying, in effect:

We'd like you to suffer personal loss for corporate gain. Neat, huh?

Thus, when change hits, a gap is created. A gap between where I'm supposed to be and where I really am.

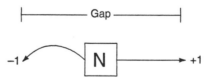

Over time, of course, that gap begins to close on its own. Employing the truism that time heals all wounds, organizations point out that, yes, we had difficulties, but now things are getting "back to normal." And the gap *does* begin to narrow; things *do* get better—that is, until another change hits,—at which point the gap widens again. Thus, in a chaotic, permanent white-water environment many organizations experience an accordion effect. Things get better and worse and better and worse, but there is never any resolution. This seesaw effect fosters mistrust and lack of commitment. Ultimately, they simply follow the organization's example and look after their own needs. The organization survives and continues to function, but as each week passes it is making itself less and less able to respond to subsequent changes that will surely come.

Managing change, then, requires working both sides of the N. Organizations and managers tend to be good at working the plus-one side because that's how they have been educated and trained. Where they need help and insight is in working the minus-one side. One manager once told his people, "If you want to have feelings, have them at home! This is a business." This manager expressed, in exaggerated form, the attitude of many people in organizations, namely, that either because "I haven't been trained, or because I am uncomfortable with upset people, or because I don't know where to begin, I would rather avoid all these messy, minus-one emotional issues and just do my job."

Such attitudes reveal a failure to realize that in a changing environment, dealing with all the issues—the messy as well as the clean—is their job. In other words, the old tape "Information is Key"—just tell people what's going on and they'll adjust—is only half true at best. There is research to indicate that, when organizations communicate just information it may help at first but quickly begins to actually hurt the effort because the organization is perceived as uncaring and machinelike.[1] Thus, in this chapter we are going to focus on communication. But this communication can be fully understood only in the broader context of our previous chapter's subject, openness.

OPENNESS REOPENED

Of the four factors necessary to success in a changing environment, openness seems like an orange among apples. Unlike communication, support, and experimentation, openness seems a little less concrete or applicable. In an organization setting, however, openness among employees, managers, and executives is absolutely essential, primarily because of its relation to trust. When I worked at Wilson Learning Corporation, we once did some research into the area of trust in order to discover: What is it? how do you get it? how do you lose it? and what are its elements? We ultimately found that trust was a function of:

- *Past history*—a track record of consistency; of doing what I say I will do.
- *Positive intent*—clearly communicating my desire to help and my regard for your best interests.

- *Openness*—honestly expressing my feelings, emotions, and concerns.

The first two clearly work hand in hand. If I express my positive intent and then follow through on that intent, I have demonstrated trustworthiness. But openness—why is that so important? I received a clear answer to that question one time when I was talking to some people in a large organization in the process of being merged with (that is, squeezed into) another organization. Speaking of her boss, one woman stated simply, "I don't trust him. I can't read him." I was curious.

"When you say can't read him, what do you mean?" I asked.

"I want to know where he's coming from," she replied. "How he feels, what his concerns are. If he has any worries."

"Why is that important?" I asked.

"Well," she answered, "I know he's got concerns and worries. We all do. So if he pretends he doesn't have them or tries to hide them, then how can we really trust anything he tells us?"

"So openness equals trust then?" I asked.

"Absolutely," she said. "If he's open and honest, then we can take anything he gives us at face value. We can act on it. The way things are now," she continued, "we can't trust information because it's changing all the time. And so, if we can't trust the information, we had better be able to trust the people who are giving it to us. Otherwise we don't really have anything solid we can go to."

This woman expressed succinctly what our research indicated was the basic relationship between openness and trust, namely that in a chaotic environment we have to trust people more than information; and that in order to trust people we need to be able to read them. If we can see that they have issues and concerns similar to ours we will feel more comfortable taking action. If they are closed, however, then we will be reluctant to commit. We will feel they are hiding something. We will choose inaction over risk just to protect ourselves. Clearly then, in a changing environment, those responsible for communication must cultivate a habit of openness.

When I explain the relationship between openness and trust to people they generally concur without reservation. But when I ask people to be more open in their organizations there is generally some reluctance. As with so many things in a changing environment, the problem is not with the idea or suggestion, but with some obstacle, some "they" or some "it," that is standing in the way; some unwritten rule that discourages a true airing of feelings, concerns, and worries. Some of the more common reasons given for avoiding higher levels of openness are:

It's not professional   It's an indication of weakness.
They don't care.   They already know how I feel.
It sounds like whining.   I don't want to be negative.
Why bother? What good   (I don't want to be a sad sack.)
  would it do?

At a strictly supervisory/management level, the most common responses are:

How can I be open if I don't agree with the change?
I need to appear confident.
I need to set an example.

From these statements, we can deduce a set of unwritten rules:

Feelings are not professional.
Expressing concerns is negative.
Worries are not businesslike.
Managers need to be positive.

Even though these rules have never been particularly helpful, they were at least tolerable and somewhat functional in a stable environment. When these rules bleed through to a changing environment, however, they break down altogether. Therefore, it is essential that these minus-one issues find expression in times of change for the double purpose of identifying the key issues and concerns and establishing an environment characterized by trust. Thus to remove the organizational bias against openness in our communication process we need to frame our openness by: (1) focusing on issues, and (2) adopting an owner rather than a victim mentality.

Focus on Issues

One way to focus on issues is simply to attach a feeling to that issue. So instead of just expressing aggregate, free-floating emotions such as worry or anger, attach those feelings to specific issues so that the statement becomes, I'm worried about this or I'm angry about that. As ridiculously simple as this process sounds, I am always amazed to observe organizations where the issues and feelings never really attach themselves to each other. If people are encouraged to state the issue and the feeling as one, however, the feeling gains a sense of legitimacy which then adds an element of urgency to the issue. The process of linking the two also forces people to identify the root causes of their reactions. The more specific the better.

Owner versus Victim

The key to openness, however, is the ability to express feelings and concerns as an owner instead of as a victim. Victim statements are characteristically "they" statements. "They did it to us," "It's up to them," "I wish they'd stop that." The extension of this orientation is helplessness, that is, "Because they did it, we're helpless." As self-defeating as this point of view is, the other side of the victim coin is even worse. If "they" did it, then who are the only ones who can undo it? The answer, of course, is them. So by taking a victim stance, we rob ourselves of the power to correct it.

The owner, on the other hand, takes a "we" or "I" point of view. "We find ourselves in the position of . . ." or "I find it frustrating that . . ." or "We need to . . ." If we shift the focus to ourselves we can seldom reverse the forces of change but we can put ourselves in the mental position of identifying options.

Perhaps the most useful aspect of the owner point of view— with regard to openness—is the answer to the question: "Is it possible to not like a change and still be an owner?" People's first response to that question is often no. If you own it, they argue, then you have to be positive and sell it to others.

"Why?" I ask.

"Because if you're not positive, you don't really own it," they answer.

This equation of owning and liking is a holdover, another bleed through, of normative attitudes. In a stable environment, the system is set, therefore advocacy is the order of the day. In a changing environment, a chaotic environment, reinventing, creating, tweaking, or even destroying, are the operative activities. As a result, to own is not necessarily to like and protect. Rather, to own is to be realistic and willing to alter, to test, or to get rid of.

In the story at the beginning of this chapter, the vice president's statements at the first meeting were classic owner statements. "I'm worried about that . . . I'm hopeful in this area . . . I think this was a mistake and I'm going to bat for us to try and right it . . . I think this is probably a good idea, but I'm not sure." He was for some things, against others, and ambivalent about still others. In other words, he didn't feel the need to necessarily defend or champion all aspects of the change. Also, he was honest about his own feelings of worry, confusion, hope, and a little anger. I am sure nobody saw his openness as a sign of weakness or disloyalty. On the contrary, they felt he was being candid and straightforward, both at an organizational and a personal level. It was only later that he switched to a more rah, rah and less open position, even characterizing his former (and very honest) openness as the musings of a sad sack.

Openness, then, is the willingness of people to disclose their feelings, concerns, worries, and hopes during times of change. Although most people will agree that openness is a good thing, the force of the normative mindset in the workplace has tended to regard such behavior as nonprofessional, unnecessary, or simply superfluous. In a changing environment, however, it is an essential element for helping people and organizations create movement. Its value, moreover, stems not so much from the comfort and catharsis it can generate (the misery-loves-company factor). Rather, the value of openness lies in its ability to foster trust, which in turn enables people to more readily act and take risks. In a sense then, although I fully consider openness a positive trait in its own right, openness as an element in communication is a means to a broader end—a leveling effect that produces a bias for mutual action without fear.

COMMUNICATION STRATEGIES

I was once involved in helping an executive frame his comments to his company's employees. The organization had just gone through a downsizing and the stated purpose of the meeting was to announce the new organizational structure. This was the third such meeting in a year; the employees were both fearful that they were going to hear the same old thing but also hopeful that maybe, this time, it would be different. As the meeting drew closer, I feared the former—that it was likely to be the same old thing. My reasons for this fear were based on the statements that the executive team was making in preparation:

"We can't tell them that, it'll only upset them."

"We need to get their commitment to the new program before we leave the room. Otherwise we've failed."

"I don't want to hear any more about how or why we let those people go. It'll only open a can of worms."

"Are the transparencies ready?"

"We've got to let them know that we haven't fumbled the ball and that we've got their best interests in mind."

"We can't share that with them until we know for sure."

"I want this meeting to clear the air so we can get on with it."

I couldn't have agreed more. They needed desperately to clear the air and get on with it. But the direction of the discussion was heading them toward—if not disaster—at least disillusionment. They were framing the meeting in very standard or normative terms. Specifically:

1. They were focusing more on what *not* to tell than what to tell.
2. They were more interested in *their* agendas, the new organization chart, than the employees' agendas.
3. They considered the meeting as a once and for all activity, that is, after the meeting it would be business as usual.

4. They wanted to bolster their own credentials for continued leadership.
5. They wanted to discourage what they called continued negative feelings.

In short, they had a classic plus-one meeting in the offing. Also, the main source of energy behind the plan was more a self-protection issue, I think, than an organizational issue. If it had been purely an organizational issue, the emphasis would have been on information and strategy—a kind of "kick butt and take names" approach. But in their discussion was a pervasive tone of self-justification; a sense that they needed to defend themselves against the implicit accusation that the current state of affairs was somehow their fault. At bottom, they had not self-managed. They had not flipped their kayaks, but were still in the grips of the need to succeed and the need to be right.

I suggested that some self-disclosure, some openness, might help, and further, that the employees could probably handle just about anything they could dish out, so why not give them all the facts, both positive and negative. They were attracted by the self-disclosure suggestion, but repelled by the idea of sharing information that wasn't totally sure.

The meeting itself was a failure. Two vice presidents came on first to warm up the crowd with some jokes and assurances. The employees were antsy, and they resented the plus-one blather they were getting. The CEO then came on and went into a 20-minute, heartrending account of the struggles he had gone through in the past weeks and months. His story took us all by surprise. I was encouraged at first. He was being open. But it went on—and on. It was a case of openness run amok. Initially, employees responded positively. But as he continued, they began to tire. Finally, the attitude became, as one person expressed it later, "Cry me a river, buddy. At least you still have a job—your same job—and a six-figure salary." The CEO's story illustrates the difference between openness and self-serving attempts to garner support through pity. The purpose of self-disclosure is not to focus others on one's problems, but rather to create a climate of mutual trust and free airing of concerns. In this case the CEO got so carried away that the employees' concerns and struggles were diminished by comparison.

After his story, the CEO bulled through the main agenda, answered a few token questions from a by now discounted group of employees, and dismissed the meeting with a sense of personal release and optimism not shared by many.

I share this horror story for two reasons: First, because it is a virtually complete list of what not to do; and second, because such meetings are actually quite common in organizations today. Now compare this experience with that of one large division of a Fortune 500 manufacturing company. This division saw the need to address a change that had been dragging on for over a year. They had thought the problems associated with the changes would go away, but they didn't. So they decided to cut through and establish a baseline; to declare, in essence, that regardless of whatever they may have done in the past, from now on they will deal with these issues proactively.

They drew up what they called "The Facts of Life," a presentation that laid out seven basic "facts" facing the organization. Several of the facts given were simply market conditions; several were facts with negative outcomes in the form of closings and potential layoffs; several were new directions which were a little vague but positive nevertheless. In all, the executives reported current conditions to the best of their ability and promised updates as things changed; they didn't pull any punches in regard to the bad news; they weren't afraid to outline a new direction even though all the details were not as yet totally clear. In addition, they assigned executive committee members to take this message to the far-flung branches across the country, and these people delivered the message, in person, with brevity, candor, and openness.

The general framework for this meeting followed the simple steps of a communication strategy which I have found effective in changing organizations. Now, when people or organizations ask me for change recipes I am always a little reluctant to respond— at least in the exact terms they want. But in the area of communication I feel confident to offer, if not a recipe, at least a format for a basic communication approach in a changing environment. The stages in this format are: framing the meeting, defining the current reality, providing self-disclosure, and outlining outcomes and subsequent steps. However ordinary and obvious these items may appear at first glance, there is a little more to it than first meets the eye. The remainder of this chapter is designed to help you understand and creatively implement this technique. For my purposes, I call it a "reframe meeting."

THE REFRAME MEETING

1. *Frame the Meeting:*   Describe the need and direction of the meeting as one of starting over or establishing a baseline.

   "The purpose of this meeting is . . ."

2. *Current Reality:*   Describe as concisely as possible the key facts of your current environment.

   "The present situation is . . ."

   "What I know is . . ."

   "What I don't know is . . ."

3. *Self-Disclosure:*   Share your own feelings and thoughts on the current situation.

   "My own thoughts are . . ."

   "I'm hopeful about . . ."

   "I'm concerned (or worried) about . . ."

4. *Outcomes:*   Define your ends and means for the future.

   "What we want is . . ."

   "How we're going to do it is . . ."

   "Why we're doing it is . . ."

   "Who it will affect, and how, is . . ."

Framing the Meeting

Whether an organization is just embarking on a series of major changes or it has been in the throes of change for a long time, there is a need, at some point, to have a meeting from which people can mark time. Some of the terms that have been used to characterize this meeting are:

- Putting a stake in the ground.
- The do-or-die meeting.
- Establishing a baseline.
- The day we cut our losses and regrouped.
- The first-day-of-the-rest-of-our-life meeting.

The actual words may vary, but the spirit of such a meeting is one of acknowledging that the change is different from changes in the past, perhaps that the organization had underestimated the scope of the changes or simply that a new direction is necessary. This meeting or communication need not be serious or heavy—although it may be—but it does serve the purpose of letting the organization know that its leadership knows what is happening and that it needs some attention.

The objection to such a meeting is, of course, that it may unduly alarm or upset people and therefore should be avoided. In my experience, by the time an organization needs such a meeting, people are already alarmed and upset, and to ignore their reactions or pretend that things are normal only makes the situation worse and fosters distrust. But if the organization's leadership, whether it be the CEO or a foreman in a factory, says, in effect, "Well, we've got a situation here that needs some attention and I want us to start doing something about it today," the result is credibility and relief. The people in the organization essentially say: "They know. They're not going to pretend or ignore us to try to sweep the issues under the rug."

Framing the meeting is a very short and simple opening which acknowledges:

- The disruption caused by the change.
- The need to address issues in a more realistic or updated manner.

Defining the Current Reality

After framing the meeting, the next most effective step is to summarize as concisely as possible the state of affairs, or current reality. Historically, the problem associated with this step has been that organizations tend to overdo it—to tell their people much more than they really want to know. More specifically, they tend to go into great detail and sometimes muse over facts and information of more interest to the organization's leadership than to the employees. I have seen people lead audiences through long and convoluted explanations of market conditions and their corporate strategy. Added to this mixture of fact and opinion is often a plus-one, candy-coated pitch to hang on, or to pitch in until the situation gets better. What is needed in this context is not a full analysis of the organization's current and future position, but rather a clear and succinct statement of the basic facts that apply directly to the audience being addressed. Later, in a question-and-answer period, it will be possible to expand on any points or areas that need further examination. But to begin, keep it focused.

Perhaps the best means of presenting this information is in bulleted form. As mentioned earlier, one organization identified what they called the facts of life, seven key points that were affecting the organization. They constituted a mixture of positive and negative, known and unknown, external and internal facts and projections. Each fact took a few minutes to explain. When the presentation of these facts was finished, the audiences had a clear and focused summary of the basic forces affecting them as well as the feeling that upper management was being candid and straightforward.

The key steps in crafting a state-of-affairs presentation are:

- Identify the 5 to 10 key facts, conditions, or developments currently affecting the organization.
- Examine each of these in terms of impact or potential impact on employees.
- Do not censor.
- Write a short explanation of each item.
- Deliver these facts to the employees as concisely as possible and allow time for questions.

I find that when I ask supervisors, managers, or executives to net out their state of affairs, they are often struck by:

- How easy it is to identify the key issues.
- How it tends to clarify the situation and often makes it look, if not better, at least more handleable and manageable.
- How much the employees don't respond negatively or with worry; but on the contrary, how much they appreciate it.

Finally it is helpful, in this portion of the meeting, to make a clear distinction between what you know and what you don't know (or don't know for sure). In that way, you can separate sure things from possible things or events in progress. By making this division clear, you will avoid misunderstandings and provide a level of comfort for yourself in dealing with unknowns.

This treatment of the current reality fulfills the need for organizational openness. Next is the issue of personal openness.

Self-Disclosure

Up to this point, the meeting we have described is basically a variant on a normal organizational meeting. It has set forth a purpose and provided some needed information. This meeting differed from a normal meeting in that its focus was on a new start point, and the tailoring of information to meet the needs of the employees, not the leadership. I have found that these two distinctions, seemingly subtle and simple, make a tremendous difference in the overall impact of the meeting, most notably on the sense of trust and honesty it generates.

What really cements this meeting, however, is the ability of the deliverer to briefly explain his or her feelings—to self-disclose. We need not go into great detail about this process; the essential elements of it have already been covered in the openness chapter and earlier in this chapter. Suffice it to say that a short self-disclosure statement is the catalyst that enables the rest of the information being presented to transcend mere intellectual understanding and attain a level of emotional/intellectual credibility. It is also wise to remember that when people display personal vulnerability, it is seen as a sign of strength, not weakness.

In preparing such a statement of current reality, first:

- Identify and describe your own feelings and emotions.
- Identify things you like, that you are hopeful about or see as positive.
- Identify things you don't like, that you are concerned or worried (or angry) about.

Then:

- Write out a concise statement expressing the facts, opinions, and feelings that seem most immediate to you.
- Deliver this information to your audience.

Nobody expects you to be positive about everything. They want you to be realistic. Therefore simply be straight about things positive and negative and try to always attach your feelings to specific issues.

Outlining Next Steps

A well-informed meeting that presents a clear statement of the current reality, accurate and up-to-date facts, and honest self-disclosure will go a long way to creating a platform, a jumping-off point for moving forward with trust and candor to address the issues of a chaotic environment. The purpose of this meeting, it must be remembered, is setting a stake in the ground. The actual details of the strategy to deal with change is best left to later meetings.

Still, there is often a need even in this meeting to at least give some general sense of what the next steps might be. Put another way, just delivering facts and feelings, although constructive, sometimes leaves people with a sense of "so what?" or "now where?" As a result, I think that a short outlining of these next steps is necessary to bring final closure to this meeting. The easiest and most effective way to accomplish this closure is to answer the questions: what, how, why, and who.

These four questions are not chosen arbitrarily. There are a number of personality, style, and learning models that identify varieties of types of people and their needs. One widely used model, the MBTI (Myers-Briggs Type Indicator),[2] for example, distinguishes sensors, thinkers, intuitors, and feelers. Other models identify their categories by different names and attributes. It is not our purpose here to recommend any model, but we can say that all of the models identify a relatively small number of distinct styles or types and then go on to talk about the unique needs of each. By specifically addressing the differences in how people process information, and using the four Myers-Briggs types just mentioned, it is possible to broadly describe an average population of people.

Type of Person	Wants to Know
Thinker—the analytical person who focuses on information, analysis and plans.	How? What's the plan? Lay it out.
Sensor—the action-oriented person who places a premium on implementation.	What? What are we going to do? Describe it.
Intuitor—the big-picture person who wants to know the context; how it all fits together.	Why? What is the purpose? Integrate it.
Feeler—the person who wants to know the human impact of the change.	Who? Whom will it affect? Anticipate the reaction to it.

As you read these, you will probably identify with all of these questions to some extent. If we were to push you, however, it is likely that one or two of these questions would emerge as more important than the others. To apply this information at a meeting of the type under discussion, simply make sure that you meet all of their various needs by addressing all four of the questions more or less equally. Specifically, think about and prepare concise statements that address:

1. "What we want is . . ." Provide a statement of outcomes or goals.
2. "How we're going to do it is . . ." Give an overview of the process.

3. "Why we're doing it is . . ." Present a context statement; the new box.
4. Whom it will affect, and how, is . . ." Explain the impact on people and departments.

Again, by allowing time for questions and clarifications, this method helps people gain a sense of what will happen next without having to go into great detail. The strength of this template, or formula, is simplicity and flexibility. People generally find it easy to use the format to craft their statements. Employee groups generally find the information useful and satisfying because it meets both their intellectual and emotional needs at that point. It also lays out a simple outline for them to respond to or to question.

Since it is a general template, it can also be adapted to the needs of the situation. For example, the flow can be crafted for a half-hour meeting or a five-minute update. This point, finally, is the most important. In a changing environment communication needs to take place on an as-needed basis, that is, more often and less formally than in a stable environment. Therefore, managers need a ready tool they can use on short notice. Moreover, people do not tire of hearing the same format repeated. On the contrary, since it meets their immediate and often urgent needs, the fact that they know the drill is an advantage, not a disadvantage.

Turn back to the outline for the reframe meeting on page 95 take a few minutes to actually frame or rough out a short statement for questions one, two, three, and four. See how it feels. People in my workshops invariably comment how it helps them to focus and organize their thoughts, as well as provide a greater sense of personal control. When you have finished, we will move from the one-to-group skills to the one-to-one skills of the support element in Chapter 5.

Chapter Five

Throwing Life Rings: Supporting People in Transition

Learn how to relate.

Alvin Toffler

Deal with it? Me? Are you kidding? You need Sigmund Freud to deal with that.

Response of a manager on being told to deal with his employees' reactions to change

I felt like a turkey. He just kept slicing pieces off me until finally— there I was—lying in a pile on the plate. Everything was accounted for. But I felt terrible.

Response of a person to sharing her concerns about a change with her boss

A mid-level manager in a large organization once confided to me, in very earnest and measured words, "The one thing that I know I didn't anticipate was the severity of the impact of this change on my staff." What struck me about his comments was his surprise and astonishment. He had been a manager for a long time. Still, the intensity of the reactions—his own included—took him by surprise. He didn't know what to think, how to react, or what to do. Later, when we talked, he responded strongly to the broken boxes idea. Thinking back, it occurred to him that although they had experienced change in the past it had always been what he called contained. But this one, he concluded, "This one broke the box."

Because of the surprise, panic, and shock that accompanies major change, organizations are faced quickly with strong, disruptive human reactions, and the need to deal with them immediately.

NEED FOR SUPPORT

In addition to communication and openness organizations must quickly address the need for support. That means applying the skill and knowledge necessary to identify and deal with employee reactions. Although there has been study and research done about loss and stress, little work has been done that directly applies to people in organizations in chaos. This chapter will introduce some of the work that has been done, and present some techniques and skills that promise to make the formidable task of support seem more approachable and ultimately doable. We begin with Jeff and Mary.

What's Wrong with This Picture?

Jeff could be anyone, but in this case he is a manager in an organization which has decided to "rightsize" two departments into one. Despite the technical jargon and euphemisms, everybody knows what this means—layoffs and job redistribution. Mary is one of the so-called lucky ones. She still has a job. It's a different job in many ways, and it will place her in a different building, but it's a job.

Mary now works for Jeff. They have never worked together before. They only know of each other by reputation; both are highly rated. After the difficult process of laying people off and getting settled in new offices, Jeff is ready to put the whole thing behind him and move on. However, Mary isn't. She is upset and has a lot of questions. She understands why the organization did what it did; she understands that the company's new direction is probably a good one. She also understands the potential opportunities for her personally. Yet she is upset.

Jeff can sense her anger and wants to talk to her. Mary is on his team now, and he wants to be aware of his people's concerns so he can help them. They meet in Mary's office.

Jeff:

Mary, I know this move has been tough for you. It's been tough for all of us, but I think the direction we're taking . . .

Mary:

Tough?! Is that all you call it? I'd call it stupid. Plain stupid, Jeff!

Jeff is taken aback by Mary's sudden flare of anger—apparently directed at him. Mary always seemed relatively calm, in control. This behavior seems out of character. Wisely, he allows her to vent, but for his troubles he gets both barrels in the face. Mary is upset about the decision to move her out of an area she was good at, into one she doesn't really know. "Oh, but you really do know . . ." Jeff begins to say and is abruptly cut off as Mary lays out a list of other issues: the people who got laid off, the need for training, the fact that her career path has been interrupted, the fact that the change also cost her a computer, and the inconvenience of the new location. Jeff takes it all in. To Mary, he looks cold and controlled. In reality, he feels totally out of control and is just recoiling from what he feels is an all-out attack. Searching for some point to begin, he focuses on two things over which he does have some control.

Jeff:

Okay, regarding the computer and the training you need. Those are issues, right?

Mary:

Yes.

Jeff:

I think what I can do is . . .

Mary:

Jeff, do you think that just getting a computer and some training is going to suddenly fix everything? Is that what you think?

Jeff is thrown off guard again. He is searching for a foothold, a place to begin to address issues and solve problems. But Mary seems to be using a bait-and-switch technique, bringing up one issue and when he attempts to address that issue suddenly dismissing it and hitting him with another. Mary thinks Jeff is impersonal and mechanical, trying to offer her half-baked, cracker-barrel advice just to shut her up. Finally, Jeff begins to get irritated.

Jeff:

Look, Mary. I'm trying to help here. I mean, in one sense, you know, you ought to be grateful you even have a job. Not that you don't deserve it. You do. But if we're going to work as a team here, we need to . . .

But Mary had already tuned him out. The words, "grateful you even have a job," gave her a surge of fury so strong she recoiled from it and went inward. Jeff finishes his appeal for working as a team. There is a pause. "Okay?" he asks plaintively. "Fine," Mary snaps. "Fine?" he asks. "Yah, fine," she answers, looking away. "Whatever you say." Jeff knows it's not fine. There is an uncomfortable pause. Taking advantage of the breather he tries again, more slowly, more empathetically.

Jeff:

Look, Mary. Believe me, I know this is difficult.

Mary:

Do you? You've always worked in this office. Do you know what it's like for me to have to work here now?

Jeff:

Downtown, you mean?

Mary:

Yes.

Jeff:

But isn't it closer to your home?

Mary:

> Geographically, yes. But now I don't have my carpool any more. And we only have one car—not that another one would do me any good. I couldn't afford the parking anyway. So now I'm getting up an hour earlier every day to take the bus. And do you realize what that does to our day care situation?

Jeff is totally at a loss. Another issue has arisen. Mary is still visibly upset. She doesn't seem to want to talk solutions. He wants to point out the real opportunities that Mary has. Wisely he decides not to. The conversation is going nowhere.

So, what's wrong with this picture? The answer has far more to do with Jeff than with Mary. It appears that Mary is behaving abnormally; that she is being unreasonable, and that Jeff is only trying to help. Actually, however, Mary is acting normally. It doesn't seem very normal to Jeff, but her reaction of anger is a normal, and potentially healthy, reaction to having the proverbial rug pulled out from under her. Jeff's reaction is partially normal. He feels he is under attack, and he is responding with a combination of fight, flight, and conciliation. The problem is that none of these responses is working for him. Indeed, they are only making things worse.

He is caught in a complex interpersonal interaction which can only be described as chaotic. Using the chaos terminology introduced in the first chapter, we can say that this interaction seems unpredictable, out of control. It seems to go in one direction and then in another and then back again. Jeff is so caught up in trying to figure out the flood of data that he cannot as yet see the patterns that are there.

Jeff will continue to be blind to these attractors, however, until he abandons his linear problem-solving recipe and focuses instead on observation and tries a few mini-plans—trial and error attempts—at dealing with Mary's reaction.

So, what is Jeff's recipe, the one that is failing so badly? And does he even know that he is using it? The answer to the second question is no. He thinks he is completely out of control. But there is a pattern—a basic response practiced by people in general, and managers in particular. This plan can be summarized simply as: protect yourself and solve problems.

This plan can be pictured as follows:

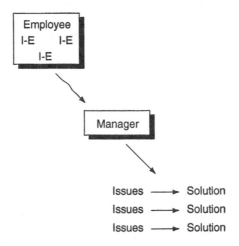

The box represents a person with some issues. Each issue has an attendant emotion. Therefore, we represent the issue/emotion as I-E. These issue/emotions result in the person being emotionally on fire, headed on a collision course with you.

In response to this confrontation, your tendency will probably be to take what, for you, is the emotionally safest route.

You will try to calm the person down (or encourage the person to express his or her concerns) and then identify the issues and propose solutions. The calming down and the issue identification stages help you feel less under attack and more in control; the solution-giving strategy plays to a human desire (the occupational hazard of managers, parents, and teachers) to be a friend, a good boss, a helpful adviser, offer sound advice, solve a problem, or, in some cases, just get the person out of your hair.

In any case, this approach, this recipe, is used often by people because it is:

- **Emotionally safe**—it focuses on issues and brings the discussion from an unproductive, emotional plane to a productive, rational plane.
- **Solution oriented**—it identifies options the person can focus and act upon.

Now, what if you are on the receiving end of this strategy? What if you are the person with the issues and the emotions? Here are some typical comments:

- I felt like I was being checked off.
- He didn't seem to want to listen to my feelings. Like he didn't care.
- I didn't want advice—especially not until he had heard all the issues.
- Don't tell me what to do! Just listen, okay?
- I felt like a turkey. He just kept slicing pieces off me until finally—there I was—lying in a pile on the plate. Everything was accounted for. But I felt terrible.

The recipient of the recipe feels, what one person described as, disqualified. Because her emotions were not acknowledged, she told me, she felt that the other person was saying, "I don't care," or "I don't want to be bothered." Because the advice was "ladled out like pancake batter," she said, "I didn't feel any ownership. I just took my pancakes like a good little girl and went off to eat them and join the clean plate club."

"What did you want?" I asked her. "To be heard," she said. "To be heard? That's all?" I asked. "That's all," she said. "To be heard."

So the question becomes, what does it mean to be heard? And further, is just being heard enough? Is there something else as well? To answer these questions is to introduce "throwing life rings," which describes helping people who have fallen into the water to get back up on the rubber raft. The subject deserves attention because, although seemingly ordinary, even mundane, the skill of being able to talk to people about their issues and concerns is one of the most important skills in managing change.

In her article, "Individual Strategies for Coping with Stress during Organizational Transitions," Susan Ashford conducted a careful analysis of techniques and strategies, official and unofficial, used during periods of organizational change. "Of the responses studied," she reports, "sharing worries and concerns appeared to be the most effective buffering response." At first, this statement may seem obvious. It is a blinding flash of the obvious. What she validated through a rather rigorous analytical process is what many people have already discovered in practice: when going through change, "sharing worries and concerns" is more than just a feel-good process of stroking and being stroked. Rather, it has the ability to focus people to motivate action. The author adds that in an organizational setting, "managers can promote the use of this coping mechanism by deliberately creating norms that encourage employees to share their worries and concerns."[1]

Encouraging people to talk, listening to them, and acting on their issues and concerns is not something that just happens, however. Beneath the rather nonspecific feel of the word *sharing* is a steel core of process, not to mention creating norms to encourage people to share. Creating norms borders on bureaucratic and seeks to make sharing official.

The remainder of this chapter addresses how this process works and what these norms might look like. More specifically, we're going to give Jeff another chance. Right now, Jeff has run into a brick wall. His attempts at empathy, his sense that he is a problem solver, and his conviction that he is a people person have gotten him nowhere. The linear plan he has been unconsciously implementing has failed. He must abandon that plan and begin looking for the strange attractors in this seemingly chaotic interaction with Mary. When we finish we will have a new set of working principles that Jeff and others can use when dealing with friends, colleagues, or employees caught in the stress of change.

THE HUMAN RESPONSE TO MAJOR CHANGE

ODR, Inc., an Atlanta-based firm that works extensively with organizations in change, defines "major change" simply as the result of the "disruption of established patterns and expectations."[2] We are all, to one degree or another, addicted to control. We like to be able to predict what will happen to us and like to have some say in our destiny. When things begin to change, we feel discomfort and anxiety. We tend to think of these changes as frustrating and irritable, even unbearable—that is, until a truly major change comes along. The point when we realize the true difference between major and minor change is when the box is broken.

There is no absolute yardstick to measure the difference between major and minor change. It varies from organization to organization and from person to person. One of the key indicators, however, is the reaction of the people in the organization. Perhaps the most common (and for me, the most revealing) comment I hear in changing organizations is, "I've never seen him act this way before" or "I've worked with her for 10 years, and this just isn't like her." There is research to support the idea that people have a reaction of choice to stress. When stress hits they habitually get mad, or clam up, or get busy. But the reaction is always the same. Under extreme stress, however, people behave differently. They get pushed through their normal response, to a secondary or backup response. The person who tends to get mad, for example, is strangely silent. The person who usually clams up, comes out swinging. Some even try to chart a predictable pattern of backup responses.

Whatever the validity of these various models and theories, one general principle seems to emerge: when people begin to behave differently than normal it means that they are under high stress. In an organization, large numbers of people under high stress equals major change. It also equals drops in morale and productivity, and seriously affects that organization's ability to cope and, therefore, to survive. Describing this condition even better is the definition of future shock as "that point in time when people can no longer assimilate change without displaying dysfunctional behavior."[3]

To be a people person, to have an open-door policy, to encourage people to share and be empathetic are no longer just the touchy-feely, nice-to-do fringe efforts. They are nothing less than survival skills for organizations involved in major change. To ignore them in favor of your strategic initiatives is to make a large mistake. More specifically, these skills are not solution-giving skills, but rather, movement-starting skills. The normative, parental response of many people and organizations is to step in and save people by giving them a solution. If you, as an individual or an organization, try to take that kind of heroic action in a rapidly changing environment, you will not only fail but burn out in the process. Your job is to change anxiety into fear thereby helping people see themselves and their options so they can begin to move. In the scenario that began this chapter, Jeff was trying to package up a solution for Mary and be done with it. He doesn't yet realize that he can't tie a bow on her situation and forget about it. On the contrary, his job is to begin using skills and creating norms to help himself and his people through the change.

The organization has moved from minor into major change—its box has been broken. Some people have been laid off; others have left of their own accord. Among those who remain there is an uncomfortable balance between a sense of optimism about what they can now become and a sense of dread about what might happen. Everything looks good now, but they know how quickly things can change. They want to believe in the permanence of the organization's plus-one scenario, yet they are also afraid that there is another shoe up there waiting to drop. And overriding all of these mixed emotions is the very real sense of loss over a host of issues regarding people, locations, jobs, machines, status, control, and teams. They are seeing other people respond to this situation differently than they normally respond. One hears statements such as, "They're coming off the walls."

In one of the first company meetings at Jeff's and Mary's organization, the president acknowledged these reactions and called for a spirit of mutual help. In what was a well-intentioned but nonspecific statement he asked people, "When you see others having difficulties in adjusting, try to help them. It's our job—your job—to deal with these situations." The unspoken response among the employees and managers was, as one person put it, "Deal with it! Me? Are you kidding? You need Sigmund Freud to deal with that!"

Sitting in the meeting that day was Jeff. As we mentioned earlier in the chapter, Jeff considers himself a people person. He has been a manager for 10 years and has always been regarded as responsive, a good manager. He took the president's request seriously and immediately thought of Mary, his newest employee. Mary is relatively young, early thirties. She is a good worker. Jeff considers himself lucky to have her. She has two preschoolers, but her new work location downtown is closer to her home than her previous suburban location. But she is clearly unhappy. In that meeting Jeff decided he would talk to Mary as soon as possible. We saw how it turned out.

Now, Jeff doesn't know whether to go back and talk to Mary or not. He is also beginning to question whether he should talk to his other people or not. What if it turns out like my meeting with Mary? he asks himself. Maybe they were right, he thinks. Maybe we do need Sigmund Freud, or the corporate human resource people. Some kind of counseling is needed. Jeff's reaction is one of the most common I run into: "I'm not qualified," "I wouldn't know where to begin."

To provide not only Jeff, but all people in organizations today, with a sense of confidence that they are in fact qualified—and that there is a place to begin—requires laying out some basic assumptions:

- People's reactions to change are for the most part normal . . . even positive. They may not always look normal or positive, but that is because they have gone unattended too long.
- Different people react to change in different ways. As a result, they require different approaches to address change.
- Managers, supervisors, and employees are fully capable of addressing each others' concerns and issues.

FOUR REACTIONS

There has been a great deal of study done in the past 20 to 30 years on people's reactions to death, loss, and change. The general thrust of this research has been to identify stages people go through in what is sometimes referred to generically as the loss process or loss cycle. Depending on the model, these stages number anywhere from four to seven and are identified with names such as denial, bargaining, anger, depression, and acceptance. Some models indicate a specific sequence; others observe a random movement from one stage to another, depending on specific circumstances. It is not our intent here to summarize these models or select one to use. It is more beneficial to simply acknowledge two general observations about people when they are under stress or caught in a rapidly changing environment: they tend to behave differently than normal and they tend to move from one reaction to another.

I have found it useful for both reducing tension and gaining a greater sense of control to see a distinction between these four basic reactions to change: *confusion, denial, loss,* and *anger.* They are similar to the basic reactions or stages identified in many models on loss but they have a somewhat different set of behaviors in an organizational setting. What follows is a brief description of the reactions in terms of: What do they look like? Why do they occur? And finally, what's good about them?

Confusion

Confusion or disorientation is the reaction that basically asserts: "I'm okay, but my world has disappeared." As a result, confused people want information and a framework to put that information into. They are saying, in effect, "How can you expect me to work if you don't give me information and guidance?" The trouble is that they want the kind of information and structure they were used to getting in a normative environment. Anything short of that level of detail and stability and they claim that their hands are tied. As a result, confusion is characterized by:

- *Constant question asking*—Continually asking questions of bosses, colleagues, and others to the point that they get caught in what I call "trivial pursuit": Asking questions for the sake of asking questions, as a nervous reaction rather than as a productive activity.
- *Unfocused action*—A tendency to scurry from one thing to another; to get involved in busywork rather than focused activity.
- *Lack of priorities*—The busywork is a result primarily of a lack of priorities; all activities seem to have the same weight.

When I talk to confused people I often discover that they are, by nature, a little more detail oriented than others. Often they are also industrious: in the sense that they want to feel active and involved. Lacking the detail and focus they need, then, they channel their energy into seeking information and being active.

What's good about confusion? Confused people are at least asking questions. They are willing to be involved and active. My experience tells me that confusion, like all the other reactions we will discuss, starts off as something normal and healthy and, then, for some reason, goes bad. An otherwise industrious and detail-oriented person begins to experience change and, true to form, goes active, wants to find out what's going on, wants some direction. If you work with this person, he or she is suddenly in your face. There is worry, there is anxiousness, there is impatience perhaps; but there is also a desire to act and resolve the situation. Now, if responded to in a positive and realistic manner this person is likely to begin dealing with and moving through the change. But if ignored or in effect told to go away, don't bother me, the confused person will likely turn to the negative side and lapse into trivial pursuit.

Denial

Denial (or withdrawal) is the response of pulling back. Often we see it when people who are normally positive and involved suddenly begin to draw back, clam up, and disappear. This is the person who has not quit and left, but is one who has quit and stayed. Often, this person was with us yesterday or last week, but has withdrawn today. This response is characterized by:

- *A false front*—Statements such as "I'm okay," "fine," "sure," or "whatever." They may even take a negative tone such as, "You're the boss" or "What do I know, I only work here." In general, however, the withdrawn person takes a go-along or no-problem attitude.
- *Withdrawn behavior*—These people tend to maintain a low profile. Often they stay in their office or area, avoid contact at lunch, and come to work and leave right on time. They may also suddenly develop a strong interest in their garden or volunteer work—something outside of work.
- *Will only do the minimum*—The primary symptom these people show is that they only do the minimum, and often only

do what they have done in the past. Even if their go-along attitude is perky and upbeat—giving the appearance of positive commitment—minimum performance often gives them away.

When I talk to people in denial I often find that they are afraid. They believe that there is a bullet out there with their name on it. As a result, they keep their head down, hoping not to be discovered. Also, withdrawn people are often unaware of their own behavior. They see themselves as involved and engaged. Only when I point out the obvious differences between their behavior now and before do they begin to see that they are acting differently.

What's good about denial?   Denial seems negative and in some cases quite serious. Actually, however, withdrawal behavior can be quite healthy—provided it is temporary. To draw back in the face of change is actually quite normal. Some people need space, they need to step back and think or look before they leap. The response of pulling back long enough to survey the landscape is often a very healthy and prudent step to take. The problem arises when the person decides to step back and then in effect says, "Say, I sort of like it back here. It's comfortable. I feel protected. I think I'll stay here awhile." At this point, an otherwise healthy coping technique has gone bad. The person is in denial and is very likely getting worse. Withdrawing behavior is insidious because people fall into it in gradual phases. Thus, they can become further and further withdrawn and not be aware of it.

Loss of Identity

Loss or, more specifically, loss of identity is a somewhat more complex reaction that may include withdrawal, anger, or confusion, or some combination of the three. The focus of this reaction, however, is the past. In an extreme form, the person is convinced that the only way to solve the problems of change is to somehow reinstate or re-create something that is gone. These people tend to have tunnel vision. They have put on blinders and see only one outcome for a given set of facts or circumstances. Thus their assessment of the state of affairs is basically correct but their conviction of what will happen is exaggerated or very narrow. This response is characterized by:

- *Exaggerated consequences*—For example, the person might say, "My job has been changed, and now my career is ruined," or "We used to do it this way, and now we've lost all our effectiveness." In general, people feeling a loss of identity draw erroneous conclusions from accurate facts. Moreover, their conviction that it won't work often becomes a self-fulfilling prophecy as they subtly (and sometimes not so subtly) sabotage the new system.
- *Focus on the past*—In an attempt to retain what is left of the past, these people tend to do the things they had done before. For example, they keep doing the old job although parts of that job have been discontinued, or they continue eating lunch with the old team.
- *Feeling devalued*—They take the change personally, focusing on the personal loss of status, influence, or identity that the change has caused. They insist that the change has caused negative and irretrievable consequences.

When I talk to people who feel loss, I get a sense of hopelessness. They want to go back to the past, but realize that they cannot. As a result, they often feel trapped. Any suggestion that there may be future options for them are met with a sense of despair. "Don't be naive," they tell me. "My life is over."

What's good about a loss of identity? However unrealistic the conclusions of the person sensing a loss of identity, this reaction starts out as a basically healthy one. To identify the positive elements, think of it in terms of: What is valuable about the past? The past contains our values, expertise, and experience. Initially, then, these people are saying not to throw out the baby with the bathwater. They are trying to protect and retain what is good and productive about the organization and their role in it. When it seems to them, as it often does, that the organization doesn't care, they will take a firm stand and insist that the past be the present mode. The basic impulse, however, is not to be rigid but to protect what is valuable about the system they've known.

Anger

Anger is the least socially acceptable and most potentially destructive of the reactions. It may manifest itself as overt active anger or covert smoldering anger. In either case, it is impossible to disguise. This reaction is characterized by:

- *Demonstrative actions*—Stomping, yelling, pounding of fists, slamming doors, shrugs, and sighs.
- *Sabotage*—Figurative sabotage in the form of being negative, ignoring directions or deadlines, bad-mouthing, not following through, and allowing things to fail; literal sabotage in the form of destroying machinery, ruining computer programs, or trashing files.
- *Enlisting support*—The angry person is not content just to stew; he or she will attempt to enlist support or get the backing of others; in this reaction, misery truly loves company.

What's good about anger? Angry people let you know what's bothering them. They may be a little more agitated than you are comfortable with and they may take it out on you personally, but they are at least letting you know what their issues are. When these issues are either ignored or discounted, then they may resort to more extreme measures. But, initially, their reaction is strong but honest.

INTERVENTION STRATEGIES (COPING TECHNIQUES)

If people react differently to change, then it stands to reason that they will also have different needs in coping with those changes. What follows is a summary of the basic differences in these coping techniques, specifically what each needs to let go of and what each needs from others.

Confusion—The Find and Focus Strategy

People who are confused need to let go of their demand for total information and act on the information they have. A changing, or chaotic, environment is by definition one in which events run ahead of information. The available information never seems like enough. Waiting for the information flow to catch up will take forever. It won't happen. Therefore, when helping confused people, whether they are your colleagues or employees, use the find and focus strategy. This is an information-based strategy to help people find the information they need, understand the limits, and focus on a plan. The key elements in this strategy are:

1. Provide information—as much as possible but also establishing that what you are giving is all there is and that you will provide more as it becomes available.
2. Provide a framework—try to create a big picture so that the information can be integrated into a larger context.
3. Provide assurances—let the person know that you intend to take the time necessary to address the issues and concerns.
4. Develop a focus, plan, or strategy—not necessarily a master plan, but a set of first steps to create a sense of structured movement.
5. Establish priorities—help the person to structure his or her action to avoid aimless or undirected activity.

Basically, confused people are open to a tell approach; they will soak up information readily. This particular approach is very similar to what I call the standard, or "Management 101," strategy. It is an information-based, tell-oriented approach. It is very easy for people to fall into this approach unconsciously. It works with confused people. As we will see, however, it will not work with the other reactions.

Denial—The Admit and Accept Strategy

People in denial need to let go of their need to be safe and comfortable. Their lack of involvement may have begun as a healthy, perspective-gaining approach, but has now become a form of escape. Extricating one's self from this state is often difficult because one may not be aware of the extent of withdrawal. Therefore, it is often necessary for others to help wake these people up, draw them out, and help them admit their withdrawing behavior and accept both the reality of the situation and their need for help. The basic elements of this approach are:

1. Make the first move—you will probably have to move first to confront the denial or withdrawal behavior.

2. Be prepared to dig in and listen—you will likely run into stonewalling behavior, such as "I'm fine" or "no problem." Be prepared to push to drive past these walls.

3. Present behavior facts—present the person with simple observations on how their behavior has changed; this prima facie evidence often helps them admit to changed behaviors of which they were unaware.

4. Identify issues—when the person trusts you and/or recognizes their own behavior, help them accept and isolate the separate issues.

5. Don't expect large jumps—withdrawn people tend to move slowly to reverse the direction they have taken; try to allow time for their momentum to increase.

The traditional tell orientation does not work for people who are in denial. Granted, they will probably nod and seem agreeable and accepting, but ultimately such activity is like the proverbial water off a duck's back. Instead, an aggressive, but caring, ask approach is needed to bring the person to confront and recognize the nature of his or her response.

Loss—The Clarify and Connect Strategy

People suffering a loss of identity need to let go of the past. The blinders of the way we used to do it or of the past in general provides a comfortable way of ignoring and sabotaging the future. Until people are able to see the new system or organization in its own right, they will not be able to recognize, much less act on, the new options. To break out of the sense of loss, people need to explore the limitations and illogic of their reaction and then begin to make connections with the new. The elements of this strategy are:

1. Create a dialogue—the most general approach is the most effective; simply ask them what they believe and why; in the process, people often come to realize and clarify the limitations of their own points of view.

2. Be patient—this technique is effective but frustrating; you have to watch someone come to a position you already recognize; you will want so badly to simply tell them.

3. Focus on their strengths—help the person to focus on what they do well and on what they may have to offer in the future.

4. Look for links—to help them make connections; to identify explicit abilities which they can apply in the new system.

Establishing a new identity can occur only when the old identity is laid aside. But only by fully exploring the old identity (instead of dismissing it) can people fully see its limitations, and then turn to establishing a new identity.

Anger—The Neutralize and Negotiate Strategy

Angry people need to let up on assigning blame and quell their sense of self-righteousness. Anger is a double-edged sword. There is almost always some justification, but unfortunately, that measure of justification often turns into full justification. The result is a zealot, a true believer whose actions can easily become destructive.

Common wisdom states that the best way to deal with angry people is to let them blow it off. This approach is essentially valid, but there are some other considerations as well:

1. Let the person vent—allow an opportunity and a forum for the person to fully vent, to express all his or her issues, and thereby neutralize the anger.

2. Manage yourself—since this venting might exceed your tolerance level, or may be directed (initially at least) at you, prepare yourself for what may be uncomfortable or seem like an attack.

3. Legitimize the anger—often when people blow off steam, their next act is to apologize. Therefore, acknowledge the anger by telling the person that "it's okay" or "I'm glad we got it out in the open."

4. Negotiate the issues—sort out the issues and negotiate fair compromises.

Anger is potentially the most destructive of the four reactions. It is essential to deal with it as early as possible before it increases and begins to cause more damage.

These four strategies make very simple but very important distinctions about, as the saying goes, "where somebody is coming from." All of them aim ultimately at helping a person get to the normative skills of setting goals and priorities and formulating plans. Before people can get to that level, however, there are intellectual/emotional roadblocks that must be removed. As we have seen, these obstacles can be defined as anger, fear of or reluctance to admit pain, a sense of having been abandoned or betrayed, and a sense of having been cut loose. If in approaching somebody having one of those reactions you are able to demonstrate that you know about or are sensitive to their particular obstacle, he or she will notice it. The basic steps provided on the previous pages are some simple guidelines about what general flow this conversation should take. More specifically, they serve as guidelines on whether you should tell or ask and, further, how to ask and what to tell—and when. The key to effectiveness in these interactions is to continually focus outwardly to see if you are meeting the needs of the person on the receiving end.

APPLICATIONS

Earlier we described Jeff's response to the prospect of dealing with other people's reactions as "I'm not qualified" and "I wouldn't know where to begin." We can now address both of those questions beginning with the second. A simple means to make an initial decision regarding how another person should be approached is to review the four basic reactions and see which one is evident. This tool functions as a pair of glasses one can put on. So instead of describing other people's reactions as "off the wall" or "running scared," one can say, "What am I seeing?" Specifically, when I look through the overlay of emotion, what are the behaviors? Is the person coming at me or going away? Is he or she angry, asking questions, withdrawing, talking about the past, engaging in busy work, or what? The intent here is not to pigeonhole but to develop what, in effect, is a working hypothesis—a place to begin.

Once I identify a place to begin, I can follow one of several general strategies, all designed to meet other people where they are. If someone is angry, I allow him to vent; if someone is confused, I try to provide information and a framework for him or her. These strategies are not magic, nor do they automatically solve problems. What they provide for the person using them, however, is a sense of control. If someone refuses to let the issues and feelings surface in spite of my best efforts and intentions to draw them out, I at least know that the withdrawal is strong and that I need to try some different approaches. If someone is angry, I know to sit back and listen, and to remind myself that although the anger may be directed at me, I am probably not the real object of the anger. In short, I am able to respond in a variety of ways to help create movement.

Once I've introduced these techniques in organizations, I commonly hear, "This doesn't seem so difficult" or "I do this with my family." Suddenly, then, the reactions I observe in others seem more normal, less as aberrations; and my actions seem less like clinical interventions and more like common sense. Their question, "Am I qualified?" is resolved in the affirmative.

In the case of Jeff and Mary, Mary is clearly angry. But under that anger is a sense of loss. We don't quite know exactly what that loss is. Jeff's job is to find out. In the following section, we're going to give him another chance, this time to move through Mary's display of anger and identify the key issues that may be causing it.

Correcting the Picture

At the beginning of this chapter we saw Jeff locked in a merry-go-round discussion with Mary. He seemed to be acting reasonably and in good faith; she seemed to be acting in an arbitrary and unfair manner. On closer inspection, however, we saw that the problem was more his than hers. Specifically, he was conducting the conversation to meet his comfort needs, not hers. He wanted to do what good managers supposedly do, namely cut through the emotions and get to issues and solutions. In other words, he wanted to push on to plus-one matters and, in the process, ignored her minus-one concerns. The result was confusion and frustration.

For perspective, think of it in chaos terms. Jeff began the meeting with the intent of working his linear plan. The attractor was a quick resolution for Mary's issues, and he embarked on a straightforward path to get there. It was soon apparent, however, that the system (their interaction) was far more complex than Jeff thought and he was soon lost, seemingly going in circles. Or better, the direction of the conversation began to gravitate toward certain issues such as the computer, training, moving downtown, and losing people; but just when it seemed to be settling on one of these issues it would veer off toward another. Jeff was then caught in the process of chasing these strange attractors—assuming each time that a particular issue was *the* attractor—only to be frustrated when it wasn't.

As long as Jeff continues to chase these issues (these strange attractors) in hopes of catching one and solving it, he will be frustrated. What he needs to seek out is not quick solutions but instead a perspective on the system as a whole. To begin this process, however, will entail some risk and discomfort. We diagrammed Jeff's unsuccessful attempts as follows:

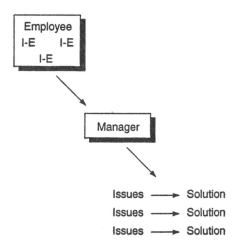

Now we can suggest another approach: the second path.

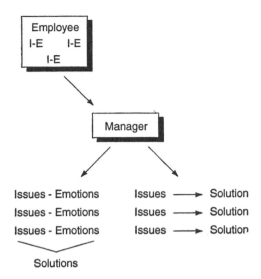

The rationale of this second path is to first identify the issues as well as the emotions that accompany each issue; and second, once the issues and emotions are clear, let the solutions fall out naturally. This approach has two fundamental advantages over the previous approach:

1. **The person with the issues feels heard**—By simply listing both the issues and the feelings, the person will feel validated. The listener does not have to agree or disagree; nor even feel any obligation to come up with solutions. The purpose is simply for the person with the issues to be able to say, "Yes. You understand."

2. **The listener has a clear division of labor**—The listener has now divided the session into two areas: First, gathering information, and second, looking for solutions. Contrast this with the previous approach in which Jeff went back and forth from issue identification to solution to issue identification to solution and so on. In that system one is condemned to simultaneously doing two mutually opposing functions, namely going wide (gathering information) and focusing down (proposing solutions). The new approach, on the other hand, allows the listener to do one thing at a time. First, focus on listening and understanding without any intent or pressure to solve, and second, looking at possible solutions to the issues as a whole.

The only possible downside to this new path is the discomfort Jeff might feel when allowing Mary's emotions to run free. Compared to what will happen if her emotions are stifled, this is a small price. In most interactions, the understanding that emotions may now be expressed freely will probably create a huge sense of emotional relief.

In the case of Jeff and Mary, the interaction using this new approach might look like this:

Jeff:

Mary, I know that you're upset by the recent events here. At least that's the way it looks to me. Am I right?

Mary:

Yes, you are.

Jeff:

Okay, so what I think might be a good idea is for you to, well, let me have it. Get the issues out on the table and then see what we can do about them. Are you okay with that approach?

Mary:

Well, yes. I guess so.

Jeff has set some basic ground rules for a discussion. He's not telling Mary how to feel or what to say. He is simply checking to see if his impressions of her feelings are correct, and then suggesting a first step in a process to get them addressed. In this manner, Jeff has outlined an open and fair way for them to proceed. There is, however, one more thing he may want to do. He may want to create a norm—a somewhat more specific set of guidelines for the discussion to take.

Jeff:

Also, Mary, let me suggest something that I think will make this thing a lot smoother. What I'd like to do first is get the issues and your concerns and feelings out on the table. I don't want to even think about solutions or next steps until we have a sense of the big picture. Then, when you're satisfied that I understand the situation as a whole, we can start looking at some ways to address them. Okay?

Mary:

Okay.

I realize that the dialogue may seem a little stilted or artificial. Part of that is because of the nature of the interaction; part of it is because of the difficulties in capturing realistic angry dialogue on paper. But I hope the intent is coming through. I have seen and been involved in enough of these kinds of interactions to know that laying out ground rules (which, in effect, tell people that you want to hear them out) will be accepted no matter how awkwardly these ground rules may be phrased. People generously recognize and respond to a legitimate invitation to play fair.

By establishing rules, Jeff has given himself permission, so that if in mid-discussion Mary demands, "What are you going to do about that?" he can remind her of their agreement not to even think about solutions or next steps until all the issues and feelings were out.

At this point, Jeff and Mary enter into the discussion. Mary is likely to unload her concerns in much the same way we saw in the first interaction. The different is that Jeff, instead of trying to chase the issues around and corner one so he can solve it, is simply listening. He may want to clarify small points as they move along, but basically his job is to enable her to get all her issues out.

Jeff:

Okay, your computer, training, the effect of the change on the department. I've got these, and we'll address them. But are there other issues or concerns?

Mary:

Well yes. The move! Putting me downtown!

Jeff:

Okay, tell me about that one.

Finally, after all or most of the issues are out, Jeff needs to summarize. How he accomplishes this task is the most important part of the interaction.

Jeff:

Okay, Mary. You've mentioned a lot of issues. Now let me see if I've got them. Let me run them back to you and you tell me if I understand what you said. Okay?

Mary:

Okay.

Jeff:

These aren't in any particular order. But one thing you mentioned was the computer. That you don't have one in your office now and that you're pretty angry about that because, if I remember, it means you'll have to run around to other offices when you want to access certain things.

Mary:

Well, yes.

Jeff:

Is angry the right word?

Mary:

Well, no. Frustrated is probably more like it. We always played musical computers in the old building. I was just lucky enough to have one of them in my office.

Jeff:

So it's an issue but not a big one?

Mary:

Not really. No.

In this conversation, Jeff is trying to identify an issue, name the emotion associated with it, and determine how important that issue is for Mary. Initially he got all the issues at roughly the same level of intensity. By naming the emotion—anger—and then checking to see if that was the right word, he has caused Mary to consider her reaction in a little more depth. As it turns out, the computer is probably a nonissue. If her main issue or issues are addressed, this one will probably disappear or take care of itself. Which begs the question: What is the main issue? The answer is: It never hurts to ask.

Jeff:

So what is—or are—the main issues?

Mary:

Well, Jeff, certainly having to get up an hour earlier to take a bus is a biggie. I have two preschoolers and getting them to day care is a real hassle for my husband and me. But I don't know what you could do about that.

Jeff:

Well, we might be able to do something with flex time, but let's keep going. You were saying?

Mary:

Well, Jeff . . . (Mary pauses.) You said no holds barred, right?

Jeff:

Absolutely.

Mary:

Well Jeff. It's you.

Jeff:

Me?

Mary:

Not you personally, but your position. We've been here about the same amount of time and I guess I feel I'm qualified and entitled to a management position by now.

This revelation took Jeff by surprise. At first he toyed with the idea of talking about his experience, why he deserved his job, or the fact that the organization was flattening its management structure—any of which would have been inappropriate, not to mention disastrous, to mention. Although he feels very uncomfortable, he attempts a response.

Jeff:

Well, I can see why that would be an issue. I've felt frustrated for a long time myself. But is it fair to say that a key concern—maybe the root concern here—is really about career?

Mary thinks for a moment and then responds almost as if she were surprised.

Mary:

Yeah, maybe it is. Or maybe it has more to do with recognition.

Jeff:

Recognition within the department?

Mary:

Yes.

Jeff:

Well, maybe that's the place to start then. When you say recognition what exactly are you talking about?

Jeff's and Mary's conversation has passed the anger and confrontation stage and moved to talking turkey; that is, two people discussing the issues as equals. They may not agree, but they will at least pinpoint the issues and eventually identify some action. We can identify some of the basic differences—and advantages—between this discussion and their initial confrontation.

- Jeff feels in control of himself. He has laid out some very basic and fair ground rules and Mary has agreed. Therefore, he can listen and try to capture the issues and emotions without feeling personally attacked or feeling the need to jump in and propose solutions.
- Jeff is identifying the issues but also is trying to identify and state what he senses are Mary's feelings about those issues. She may agree with the word he chooses or change it. In either case, he is not telling her how she feels; simply clarifying it. This technique is the single most important skill in the interaction. The result will be Mary's conclusion when it's over that, "I was heard. You understand me." This fact alone will take away the edge on Mary's anger and the defensiveness in Jeff's response. It will allow them—even if they don't fully agree—to at least identify options.
- Mary feels more and more free to express her true emotions and concerns. As a result, these issues and feelings become grist for the problem-solving mill rather than hidden obstacles to communication.
- Given the free expression and defining of the issues and attendant feelings, the solutions are more likely to fall out as obvious next steps rather than taking the form of Mary's demands or Jeff's decisions handed down from on high.

In retrospect, then, what seemed at first to Jeff as a chaotic interaction with Mary was not so chaotic after all. There was a turbulent flow of emotions and issues swirling around both of them as they strove to find some kind of resolution. In addition, there were a number of false starts and stops as Jeff tried occasionally to chase down an issue and trap it. But as the interaction continued, it became apparent to him that the issues were not the issue. At that point he had another chance in the form of a new approach. He was then able to free himself of the need to chase issues and could basically just gather in the whole. This shift helped him feel more calm and more in control. It also gave Mary the sense that somebody was really listening and that the conversation was going somewhere. Jeff and Mary were aware that the root cause of her reaction—her real goal—had something to do with career, or even recognition.

I am not suggesting that people's change issues can all be traced back to deep issues, such as recognition. On the other hand, I am quick to remind that many of people's change issues do stem from issues such as recognition. As we saw in Chapter 3, "Flipping Your Kayak," real goals in the form of needs to succeed, be loved, and be in control are often the root motivating factors in people's reactions to change. As in the case of a person like Mary, the bottom-line issue might be the sudden disrupting of her and her husband's schedule and day care arrangements; or it might be worry about her own job security; or it might well be a career-related and personal frustration related to being recognized for her abilities. In any case—whatever the base issue—there is a need to identify it. Whether it is easily solvable or not is not as important as getting it out in the open. Also, Jeff need not feel like he has to come up with a solution. As mentioned earlier, the primary job of people helping other people is to be a movement starter, not a solution giver. Once people see clearly the full scope of their issues, the solutions or options tend to suggest themselves quite naturally.

What we hope to have described in most of this chapter is a very basic set of communication skills. I make no excuses for this approach, however, because I am continually reminded that the core of the work I do always comes back to the bedrock of listening and communicating, to putting one's own personal agendas aside long enough to hear somebody else's agendas and concerns. In my wallet, I carry the following quotation by TV journalist Diane Sawyer:

> Michael J. Arlen, a wonderful writer, said to me once that the greatest act of love is to pay attention. That's so true. I think the one lesson I have learned is that there is no substitute for paying attention.[4]

Certainly in a changing environment where people's loss of control is inversely and increasingly proportionate with their rising tension, the ability to pay attention and listen has never been more important.

No book on change that truly wants to be helpful—no matter how eloquently it may handle the subjects of strategic thinking, creativity, and the like—is complete without addressing in some way the workhorse of change: communication.

We hope we have added to the basic subject of communication some original insights and approaches in the form of the two paths diagram. The book *Aftershock: Helping People through Corporate Change*,[5] by Steve Buchholz and myself, is devoted almost entirely to the techniques and applications of the communication process in a changing environment. My intent here is to home in on the primary obstacles to the success of that process, namely the human penchant—whether you are a boss, parent, teacher, friend, or colleague—to protect yourself emotionally and to feel you must have the answer to provide a solution.

CREATING NORMS

In the conclusion of her article on coping with stress in organization change, Susan Ashford described coping mechanisms that offer long-term payoffs. "Feelings of personal control, the ability to tolerate ambiguity, and sharing one's worries and anxieties," she states, "buffered the immediate stressor effects, but also were associated with reduced stress six months following the transition."[6] I think that there is a cause-and-effect relationship between these elements, starting with the sharing of worries and anxieties. Getting these issues and concerns out in the open and identifying them results in a greater feeling of personal control. More specifically, the person is not controlling the situation; rather, by being able to identify clear options the person feels more in control in the midst of the situation. The individual then has a sense of movement and direction, and as a result, is able to tolerate more ambiguity. He or she is less likely to demand that things suddenly resolve or right themselves, and can accept new developments as a natural part of the flow.

Organizations tend to not do a very good or at least not a very consistent job of dealing with what Ashford calls worries and anxieties. The primary reason for overlooking this important function is simply that there really hasn't been a need for it until relatively recently. Normative and relatively stable organizations certainly had their share of upset and anxious employees, but most concerns could be handled by traditional coaching and counseling techniques or by simply ignoring them. If something or someone got really out of hand, there were crisis-intervention measures, and in some organizations, on-staff human resource staff counselors. Also, there have always been those people—managers and employees—who possess and regularly apply the very techniques we are describing. For many years, then, the business of businesses, hospitals, schools, and organizations in general went on, operating in a relatively controlled in-box mode.

When, in the 70s and 80s, change became more of an issue and the organizational boxes began to break—when, as Toffler put it, "the future arrived too soon"—the pain curve began to rise. One of the earliest symptoms recognized was stress. People had always talked generically about the rat race and the stress associated with it, but it was not until the 70s and 80s that stress with a capital S became a bona fide issue, complete with causes and effects, and books offering techniques to cope with it. For the most part dealing with stress was still a personal issue, not an organizational issue. Organizations recognized its existence and even agreed that it affected performance, but still viewed the subject as largely a matter for the individual to deal with, but not on company time. Certainly it was not written into the job descriptions of managers to spend time specifically addressing employee stress issues.

But what if stress is so widespread that it becomes the rule rather than the exception? How should an organization respond when three out of four of its employees are exhibiting symptoms of stress? This is where what I choose to call the "stress paradigm" begins to break down.

The stress paradigm advocates that when you experience stress, take action to relieve it by changing your lifestyle and removing the stressors. But what if an entire organization is under prolonged stress? According to the stress paradigm it would have to take heroic measures and change the organizational lifestyle in an attempt to cure the problem. This tactic would surely fail, however, because the organization has so little control over the primary stressor, the pace of change—which, by the way, only shows signs of increasing rather than decreasing. To put the focus on the stress, then, only plays to a normative mindset.

Thus the primary obstacle to dealing with change is the existing culture and its norms. This culture may pay lip service to supporting its employees, but it has difficulties allowing time off to deal with what looks like a personal problem. One manager once stuck his job description in my face and told me, "This is what they pay me to do around here. It doesn't say anything on here about listening to a lot of bellyaching—doesn't say anything about doing a lot of hand-holding." Another manager, responding to the idea of normalizing the addressing of worries and concerns, told me, "Oh, we already do that. People can come to me any time they want. We're pretty open around here." When I talked with this person's employees I discovered it was true; many felt she was very approachable and responsive. Others, however, did not. A few didn't really feel comfortable talking about things like that. One person just didn't like her. In still other organizations, the prevailing attitude is "don't crack, just work; we haven't got time for your personal problems." The press of business is too great as it is, the argument goes. There is too much to be done and too little time. If you want to have a personal crisis, have it on personal time—preferably over a weekend.

In general, organizations are very aware of the problem but don't see how they could ever really address it. Whenever I talk to organizations about the need to focus on the "people breakage," I hit a nerve. People sit up and say, "Boy, is that true. We have things going on here you wouldn't believe!" But when they see that the strategy to address these issues is largely a basic application of communication skills to a changing environment, they sometimes seem a little disappointed. They were expecting a pill and what they see is a process. As a result, in many organizations the approach receives a resounding initial endorsement only to die for the lack of a second.

If the prevailing attitude in an organization is "Stop bellyaching and buck up!" or "Have your feelings at home," or if individual persons are of the opinion that "this is none of my business" or "I don't have the skills; what you need is a professional," then the need for an organization purge valve will only increase. Even if the prevailing attitude is "my door is always open," the question becomes, "Yes, but do you have a norm? Do you have an established procedure for listening to concerns? Do you have a method or set of techniques to conduct that interaction?" Good intentions and general feelings of openness will not suffice—not in a chaotic, changing environment.

What I think is both necessary and possible for organizations is to move off the stress paradigm and look at people's responses to change as being basically normal reactions that need to be addressed on an ongoing basis rather than as emotional abnormalities that need to be "fixed." Accepting ongoing reactions to change as normal, then, and not as stress-related abnormalities to be isolated and treated will help to build a work culture that continually responds and supports itself.

I Have a Problem, I Need Your Help

One organization I am familiar with established a support norm as a result of a poor actor in a bad video. In the video, seen by many in the company, an actor delivered the line, "I have a problem, I need your help" so poorly that it became an in-house joke. People continually mimicked the line. Everybody had a good laugh. But over time a strange thing happened—the line became a very positive and functional signal that a person did indeed need some help. Without going into detail, eventually it became a code phrase—a shorthand way for any person in the organization to call for assistance. As a result, when someone today says, "I have a problem, I need your help" everybody knows what it means: Stop what you're doing, listen to me, this is serious. Also, the phrase is not used lightly. People don't abuse or overuse it. Finally, a corollary phrase, "You have a problem and you need some help," also came into use as a means for one person to reach out to someone else. The end result of this evolution is that now the phrase, hackneyed though it is, is an accepted, normal way to express concern that, when uttered, will result in an interaction not unlike the one we presented. This organization's story happens to be a case of support developing spontaneously in response to what was at first a joke. But to more consciously establish a normalized method for allowing people to express worries and concerns and issues, let me pull together some of the ideas from the last few chapters and suggest the following general process:

1. **Create a context.** Either through training or via a reframe meeting (as outlined in Chapter 4), establish the new context you are operating within, as well as its new rules. This step may also include using the growth curve, the chaos concept, or some other organizational development model. The purpose of this step is to create a common base of knowledge and a common set of expectations, including the idea that individuals need and ought to be able to get support.

2. **Introduce a support skill.** Using the intervention strategies discussed earlier in this chapter or ones consistent with the principles of this chapter, train managers, and ideally also employees, in the use of this skill. At the very least, create a companywide (or departmentwide) awareness of the purpose and the process of this skill.

3. **Normalize the support skill.** Either via the use of a code word or phrase (or in some other creative way) establish a mechanism whereby people can both put out a call for support or reach out to support somebody else. (I have a problem, I need your help/you have a problem, you need my help.)

4. **Implement the support skill.** To the extent it is logistically possible, the manager should use the technique with all direct reports. This start-up may be both awkward and time-consuming at first. The effort is worth it because people learn very quickly that you are serious. The technique will build credibility and yield results.

This process is straightforward and effective, but also demanding: When practiced, the organization gives to the sometimes soft notion of support a steel core. The results are increased morale, higher levels of trust, and greater measures of focus and direction.

CONCLUSION

In terms of chaos theory, the swirls, eddies, and currents in a turbulent river are amplified and unchecked results of riverbed abnormalities such as submerged rocks and dead trees. Mapping these abnormalities, much less calming the turbulence, is an impossible task. Many organizations feel the same kind of helplessness when it comes to dealing with issues of change, especially the people issues. The elect instead to hunker down, ride the rapids, and hope they make it. Dealing with personal issues isn't nearly as chaotic as it may seem, however. What may appear at first to be deeply submerged emotional rocks turn out to be surprisingly accessible. Once people understand that there is a method and some procedures in place, to aid them and help them identify options, they are generally more than willing to cooperate.

Taken together, the application of skills of openness, communication, and support provide a powerful thrust to move the organization from minus one to the establishment of a resilient change culture. In the next chapter we move to the final skill needed, experimentation. Because of its scope, covering the entire field implied by experimentation is impossible. There are numerous books and materials on creativity, innovation, and idea application, each covering only a portion of this topic. In the spirit of focusing on key applications, our contribution to this subject is to suggest ideas and techniques for establishing a base for the creation of an experimenting organization—a learning organization.

Chapter Six

New Strokes: Creating a Learning Organization

Learn how to learn.

Alvin Toffler

Learning organizations are possible because, deep down, we are all learners.

Peter Senge
The Fifth Discipline

P erhaps the most prophetic of Alvin Toffler's three keys to dealing with future shock was his admonition that we must "learn how to learn." Implicit is the suggestion that the way we learn now isn't good enough—isn't quite up to the task at hand. I think he is right. Although they pay lip service to the need for new ideas and the value of learning in a changing environment, organizations very often behave like an immune system: attacking any outside ideas or influences that aren't part of the body. They avoid making changes in their basic curriculum—their basic approach to learning—because of what they see as the more pressing issues of a chaotic environment.

Ironically, of course, just the reverse is true. The pressing issues of the chaotic environment have elevated learning from a mere function to a survival skill. They call into focus the need for what is being called a "learning organization."

THE LEARNING ORGANIZATION

In one sense, learning organizations are nothing new. Most existing organizations have been learning organizations at one point in their history, generally in their formative stages. During that time, they encouraged and were open to new ideas; they may have had a strong leader who encouraged innovation and risk; they didn't have an established organizational or intellectual infrastructure to get in the way, and they had nothing to lose. Trial and error was a way of life.

In a transformative or changing environment, however, two fundamental things are different. There is an existing organizational and intellectual structure in place which for reasons of habit, power, and money, will resist ideas, changes, and efforts that do not show an immediate benefit or profit. Second, by not being open to new ideas and change, these organizations have a great deal more to lose in the long run than a start-up company.

In this chapter I want to outline some of the basic skills necessary in a learning organization. Specifically I want to deal first with what a learning organization has to know or accept and then move on to what it must do. In terms of knowledge and attitude, a learning organization today must recognize:

1. The nature of the changing environment.
2. The existence of opportunities amid the chaos.
3. The force of the system in obstructing change.

At first glance, there is nothing new on this list. It looks like a fairly standard set of attributes. But there are some new twists in it.

The nature of change.   First you must understand that most organizations are familiar with the effects but not with the nature of change. They see only too clearly the chaos and upheaval. But in their efforts to deal with these shocks by attempting to stabilize the environment, they ignore the ongoing, self-adapting, and unpredictable nature of that environment, and thereby set themselves up to be shocked again.

The situation in which organizations find themselves is not unlike Woody Allen's famous story about playing the cello in his high-school marching band. No sooner would he sit down and play a few notes than the band would begin to pass him by. He would then have to quickly stand up, move his chair and his cello forward, sit down again, furiously play a few notes, stand up again, move forward. And so on.

Like the cello player, many organizations are used to implementing programs based on the assumption that the organization or the problem is standing still. As such, they do too much planning and not enough adapting. Although people intellectually understand the ever ongoing and accelerating nature of change, their mental and organizational systems have not yet responded to it. In other words, they are formulating strategies to deal with the effects of change and not the nature of change.

Opportunities.   Regarding the second point, recognizing opportunities, one can listen to Tom Peters and others only so many times before one is weary of hearing about the opportunities inherent in change. In fact, in the corporate lexicon, the word opportunity has replaced problem on the most-hated list. The last thing anyone wants to hear nowadays is, "Say Pat, could you step into my office for a moment. I have an opportunity for you."

Ultimately, however, Peters is absolutely correct. The opportunities present in a changing environment are much greater than those in a stable environment. Some people instinctively recognize this fact. In virtually every organization I deal with, I inevitably run into someone who tells me: "You know, Harry, I actually like all these changes. Things are so screwed up around here that I can do things I've always wanted to do and there's nobody to stop me." These "opportunity-ists" are the exception, however. More people are focusing not on opportunities but on the third point.

The System.   In response to change, overwhelming numbers of people have taken on a victim mentality, saying: "Yes, we know all about change and the need for innovation. Don't tell us. Tell them." With this statement, they take the classic stance of the victim, the "they orientation." They did it. Talk to them. It's their problem. Victims not only give away their power but condemn themselves to self-righteously waiting for someone to give it back.

CORRECTING THE COURSE (TRUE EXPERIMENTATION)

The bottom line for any would-be learning organization is nothing short of radical. The organization's job is to change its structure; the individual's job is to change his or her attitudes. Such changes are virtually impossible to implement, however, because they require the organization and the individual to make huge shifts—which neither is likely to do. But these changes are much less impossible if the organization and its individuals can agree to some small measures—aimed at generating concrete ideas that will help the organization respond to and take advantage of the change.

Unfortunately, this suggestion to focus on individual ideas rather than the big picture seems to fly in the face of much of the current organizational thinking. In organizations today, we are encouraged to think strategically, not tactically. Or better, we distinguish between those who think strategically and those who (only) think tactically. We are encouraged to thrive on chaos, foster quality and leadership, and create our futures. In a period when our time-honored, normative systems are decaying, we call for new and bolder systems to replace them. In organization after organization I see the effects of this clarion call. People cast aside their crutches and hobble to the front of the auditorium, calling out "Yes, I want to be a strategic thinker! Count me in!"

In this flurry, people tend to forget that true learning doesn't begin with strategies; it begins with ideas and actions. Though it may be uncomfortable to an organization that prefers predictability and systems by nature, and mundane to people who want to define learning esoterically, true learning organizations:

1. Focus on ideas.
2. Build specificity.

Although greatly in need of explanation and elaboration, these two attributes go to the heart of the issue. They provide a simple context and a bias for action. In this chapter and in the final chapter, I want to focus on some basic ideas and skills that will help organizations increase their ability to tolerate and practice true experimentation.

Focus on Ideas

A learning organization focuses on ideas, not solutions. It concentrates on first steps rather than master plans. It looks for new directions rather than radical breakthroughs.

A learning organization may or may not have a solid sense of where it is going, a vision. More importantly, it knows what it doesn't know, namely, the exact route it plans to take. Its job therefore is to discover that route. Thus, it not only values but relies on ideas that will take it where it's going. It expects that certain of these ideas will fail, but from these failures will come new and more focused ideas. A learning organization, finally, is always open to the possibility that ideas can alter a vision or create a new one.

Formative, entrepreneurial organizations are learning organizations by their nature. Normative organizations are learning organizations against their nature and therefore must constantly fight to keep a part of themselves in a true learning mode. Transforming, changing organizations are learning organizations—or else. At the very point when they are looking for some stability amid the chaos, they must choose to experiment rather than pull back.

The power of an idea.   I once attended a creativity conference in Key West, Florida. The organizers of the conference invited a wide variety of experts from the business, education, and scientific worlds. Either through luck or Key West in February, a good percentage of the experts were able to attend, making the conference a kind of creativity honor roll. One of the attendees was a very successful vice president from AT&T and Bell Labs known for his impressive track record as an innovator. He was scheduled to give a talk the title of which implied (to me, at least) that he would divulge the secrets of his success.

He began by saying, "In my career at AT&T and in the Bell Labs I have had five good ideas." Then he paused and rephrased that, saying, "Well, four good ideas anyway, and one pretty good idea." He then went on to summarize his career in terms of five simple ideas. "The first idea," he explained, "was color." He paused as the audience collectively asked themselves, "Color?" The executive explained how, in the 50s, he had suggested a four-color coding system for different telephone lines. After his initial explanation, the idea hardly seemed that profound or original. It seemed quite ordinary and obvious. Only after further explanation did we see how really original and influential—and profitable—this idea was. His other ideas were similar—very simple, commonsensical and seemingly obvious suggestions. Each one of them, however, was a seed for a vast and far-reaching system which was subsequently developed to implement the original idea.

What struck me about his presentation was that he recognized and described his success in terms of ideas, not systems. He was aware that at some point in time someone needed to get, and then grow, the seed of an idea. It was not a time for planning and management—or even vision. Rather it was a time for insight and faith. As a result, he had developed the habit of responding to change by trying to come up with a new idea, not a new system. He closed his remarks by saying that as he approached retirement (he was near 65) he would consider himself lucky to get just one more good idea.

Since hearing that talk, I have always, when listening to people or organizations talk about their successes, tried to identify the role that ideas played in those successes. It is sometimes difficult to identify these root ideas because they have been absorbed and lost in the systems they have spawned. But eventually they pop out, and in most cases they number five or less. My former employer, Wilson Learning Corporation—one of the largest and most successful training and development companies in the world—owes the bulk of its success to three ideas (actually, two ideas and a good decision). Amid the scores of other ideas and directions the company took in its first 25 years, those three ideas accounted for the company's identity, the basis for its methodology, and 70 percent of its sales. In my own life, I once determined that I had three good ideas. I have since scaled that back to two. One of the ideas, a simple explanation I came up with when I was a graduate student, enabled me to create for myself a competitive advantage as a writer/photographer (my livelihood when I was in graduate school). I parlayed that idea into the core concept of my doctoral thesis, a set of successful approaches to video writing, and the basis for a discovery-learning approach to instructional design and development. Although I am still over a decade shy of 60, like the AT&T vice president, I would be grateful to have just one more idea like that one. It might carry me to retirement.

What is an idea? An idea is a suggestion, a simple model, a hunch, an adaptation, a new direction, a pet theory, an unlikely connection, a logical conclusion, an obvious relationship, or any number of other insights or applications. The latest version of the "Ten Most Important Ideas in History" list does not include the Pythagorean theorem or Freud's notions about the id. Rather, it includes such things as the wheel, the stirrup, the alphabet, and movable type.

Most people do not need to be convinced about the power of an idea. Indeed, the force of ideas is one of the axiomatic beliefs of our culture. Because it is axiomatic, however, people don't think about it very much, and as a result, tend to focus on systems rather than the ideas that spawn them. Consequently, during periods of change, people and organizations see their normative and productive systems failing and immediately look for other systems to replace them. They forget that new systems do not just suddenly appear, do not spring fully grown from the head of Zeus, but grow from ideas instead.

The notion of nurturing a new idea from scratch, however, is a frightening prospect. "We don't have enough time for that," they catastrophize. "We have to have a new system—up and running—and soon!" In reality, of course, that fear is clearly false. Their systems will not disappear tomorrow. True their current system is in decline and needs attention, but there will be a transition period, a window of time in which to generate ideas and to experiment.

Consequently, the AT&T vice president's focus on good ideas struck me as a good starting point. An organization's most effective means to innovation, or in this case to create a learning organization able to cope with change, are a function of its ability first of all to identify and nurture good ideas. If done properly, the systems will follow.

Postscript.   All this talk of ideas is well and good, but there is a problem. Although nobody is against new ideas, all too often nobody is for them, either. D. H. Lawrence put it succinctly when he wrote, "The world doesn't fear a new idea. It can pigeonhole any idea." What "the world fears," he says, is "a new experience."[1] The same can be said for organizations and people. They spend a lot of time, especially in times of change, "ideating" (or as one manager put it, "idioting"). But they are loath to dig in, act, or experiment from the bottom up. Such activity seems too mundane and limited. They would rather, as Michael Beer, Russell Eisenstat, and Bert Spector put it, begin with "knowledge and attitudes," believing that changes in these areas will "lead to changes in individual behavior." Not so, the authors say. "The most effective way to change behavior," they write, "is to put people into a new organizational context, which imposes new roles, responsibilities, and relationships on them." Further, they "must learn from innovative approaches coming from [people] closer to the action."[2] In short, in order for ideas to work, organizations need to build specificity.

Build Specificity

Ideas die for a variety of reasons. Some die because they don't make sense or seem too risky. Others die because they don't have champions in high places or because nobody understands them. Still others die because they aren't fully fleshed out and will therefore require time to develop—time which the organization says it doesn't have. Finally, ideas die because they don't conform to a particular format or a particular philosophy.

Recently I was involved in writing a proposal for an organization competing for the Malcolm Baldrige Award. Our ideas, we were told, had to be phrased in a particular language, and the proposal written in a particular format. "The ideas we're presenting," we explained, "are just that—ideas. If they are accepted then we can talk about which ones, and to what extent, they will tie to the quality specs of the Baldrige Award. But right now, they don't fully fit those categories."

"No," we were told. The proposal must follow the guidelines. "Even if in some cases the guidelines don't apply?" we asked. "They must apply," came the terse reply.

Organizations in general—but particularly organizations in change which have the least to gain from this kind of reductive thinking—tend to demand that ideas jump through certain hoops before they are worthy of consideration. They tend to miss the point that true ideas don't always know exactly where they're going or may have a certain logic and inner coherence of their own outside established parameters of evaluation.

Because they fail certain organizational tests, these ideas are often not allowed to become specific. They are not allowed to define themselves in their own terms. They are not allowed a pilot, trial, or demo to test their assumptions. Thus, many innovations, pet ideas, and suggestions from workers in the trenches never see the light of day or, if they do, die for lack of a second.

As a consequence, no learning takes place and the organization continues its own unique form of neurosis—trying the same things over and over again, expecting different results. To be a learning organization, therefore, requires that it not only encourage ideas, but establish some method to allow those ideas to take shape, to test themselves—to become specific.

Woodward's First Law. In a moment of rare inspiration, I was once moved to postulate what I call Woodward's First Law, which states: "It is easier to react to something than it is to react to nothing." The occasion was a meeting, the stated objective of which was to react to some new ideas regarding a customer service program we planned to develop. Our company—a training and consulting organization—had an existing customer service offering but it was shaggy and outdated. With the upsurge of interest in customer service, however, we decided to upgrade and build a new cutting edge product.

We talked a great deal about customer focus, internal customers, culture change, and survival in an information-age service culture. Everybody agreed that this was the heady stuff of which blockbuster products are made. But what, specifically, were we talking about? In the terminology of my law, the answer is: we were not reacting to something, we were reacting to nothing—nothing but abstractions and vague notions.

When I suggested we back up and look for some concrete ideas, models, techniques, or practices to try out—a core of beliefs and skills to actually attain customer focus—I was told, "that is product development's job." "We are product development," I reminded them. "You're not thinking strategically, Harry" I was told. "If we want to compete in the more sophisticated and changing business culture, we have to think more strategically and let someone else do the actual development." In this case, strategically meant that we had to develop marketing strategies. So forget about ideas; let somebody else do that. Develop a marketing plan. Those were our orders.

So we, the erstwhile product-development dons, received a crash course in marketing and in developing business plans. Within a month we were responsible for presenting a three-year plan to upper management. In light of the unpredictable environment not to mention our lack of marketing expertise, these proposals—presented with multicolored overheads and research-based financial projections—were nothing less than pure fiction. But they looked good; and they were strategic.

At that time, our company was suffering the ill effects of change. Like many changing organizations, its growth curve was peaking and flattening and threatening to go down. Its profits were down, its reputation was slipping, its organization was shifting, and its leadership was looking for a new system, an answer, a savior. The flavor of the month (that month) was marketing—and distribution. Never mind the ideas, we were told, but focus on a new marketing system.

What was needed was not a savior system, but a new idea. In order to get this idea we would have to muck around a little and see what, if anything, appeared. And if it did appear, we would have to be ready to accept it and examine it. No matter how strange it looked, how simple it seemed, or how divergent it appeared, it would have to be given its day in court.

In other words, we needed a corporate attitude-shift, not a new marketing strategy. We would have to develop an attitude that valued an idea enough to allow it to build specificity. Then, having built enough specificity for it to stand on its own, it would qualify as something, something we could challenge, build on, alter, and if necessary, reject. But at least it would be something rather than nothing; and by either accepting or rejecting it, we would be making progress. However, our company had ceased to be the learning organization it once was. As a result, any new ideas requesting admittance would have to come through the back door.

Postscript. Building specificity goes against the grain for many organizations, especially organizations in rapid change who regard building specificity as "diddling." "When what we need," they say, "is strategy and vision." But as Beer, Eisenstadt, and Spector put it: "Successful change efforts focus on the work itself, not on abstractions."[3] They focus on the ideas of people "closer to the action." Thus, valuing and building specificity is one of the key skills of a learning organization, a skill that changing organizations will have to relearn. There are numerous models and systems on creativity and problem solving that can be useful and later in the chapter I will present a technique that I have found to be effective. We should note that before my or any other method can fully meet the demands of a chaotic environment—before it can fully attune itself to the search for strange attractors—it must acquaint itself (or better, reacquaint itself) with its own inherent learning and connection-making capabilities.

OUTSIDE-IN AND INSIDE-OUT

Our discussion of learning begins with a distinction between outside-in and inside-out.

Outside-In

A purely outside-in approach, whether in learning, management, or even parenting, is to shoot something at or lay something on somebody else, in hopes that enough of this something will filter down, soak through, or sink in, and cause that person to act and/or think in a certain way.

Inside-Out

A purely inside-out approach attempts to somehow get inside the person, and by building on an existing knowledge base, hook into an existing value system, or validate an existing set of experiences—and thus, cause the learning and motivation to grow from the inside out.

In its application, the outside-in approach is efficient, logical, and predictable—but can also be academic, and heavily tell-oriented. The inside-out approach generally results in something more personal and useful but, from the learning or application point of view, is less predictable, more difficult, and takes longer.

Northrop Frye states:

> A true teacher is not primarily someone who knows instructing someone who does not know. He is someone who attempts to re-create the subject in the student's mind.

In this sentence, Frye has summed up the outside-in/inside-out distinction more succinctly than anyone I know. To "re-create the subject" in the learner's mind is not only working from the inside-out, but also assumes that there is something in there in the first place—something to build on as well as some things that might get in the way.

Frye goes on to say:

> To accomplish this involves a strategy to get the person to recognize what he already potentially knows; which includes breaking up the powers of repression in his mind that keep him from knowing what he knows.[4]

Here is the inside-out approach at high tide, searching the learner's mind for potential connections as well as obstacles. To implement Frye's strategy in an organization would involve the valuing of its employees' abilities and experience. It would also have to take into account any gaps or preconceptions that might, as Frye says, keep a person from knowing what he or she knows. Certainly it would require specific knowledge of current conditions and business problems.

One major manufacturing company drew on the personal knowledge of its employees in a very simple but effective way. The president visited one of the company's plants in the Carolinas. He told the workers that the company would make more money if it just took the money it was putting into their plant and put it in the bank to draw interest. This got their attention. It was not a threat; simply a fact. He said he was looking to them to figure out ways to save money, and also to improve certain processes. In swift strokes, then, he transformed a standard-operating-procedure plant into a learning organization with a vengeance. Immediately, workers identified all sorts of cost-cutting measures. They went on to devise process improvements. Most important, the organization made it normal to look for corrections and ideas, and then take the time to explain and test them out. In the meantime, it was educating the workers regarding big picture issues such as market needs. The result was many good ideas, some of which were implemented. Others were discarded because, despite their inherent value, they did not directly benefit the organization overall.

The result of this process is not only learning, but delight. The process of making connections, seeing possibilities, and discovering one's own successes or errors is not only useful, but intrinsically and personally rewarding.

This process, the producing of personally and organizationally useful knowledge and applications, is what a learning organization is all about. It depends on a hard framework of knowledge, the organization's and individuals' abilities, and an explicit understanding of business problems and issues. It focuses on producing a fluid inner core of ongoing insights which are then applied against the larger problems and issues. It thrives to the extent it can give its employees permission and support to formulate, define, and apply their ideas.

But we're getting ahead of ourselves. Before examining the framework for testing ideas, we first have to focus on how the ideas arise in the first place; how they germinate on the inside and then move out. We begin this examination at an unlikely source—humor.

HUMOR IS A FUNNY THING—THE POWER OF CLOSURE

Humor is a funny thing. Everybody has a sense of it, more or less. Most people wish they had more of it. We all enjoy it. But what is it? Like creativity and love, humor is difficult to define. Some people define it as something that makes you laugh; others as a light bulb going on. Actually it's both, and for that reason it is very important to a learning organization.

The word *humor* itself immediately conjures the idea of funniness—telling stories and jokes. In a learning situation, humor is often used superficially as an ice-breaker or comic relief, or more substantively as a means to put key ideas into perspective or enable discovery. Even at this substantive level, however, we have still not plumbed the depths of humor's potential to enable learning. We need to go deeper. To do that, we need to introduce the concept of closure.

The dictionary defines *closure* as bringing something to a conclusion or an end. If you move down a few definitions, however, you may find in your edition one that reads something like:

Closure: The process of mentally adding something that is missing.

Based on the discoveries of Gestalt psychology, closure is the act of creating a whole from an incomplete series of parts; making a connection between things that may at first seem unrelated.

What is this?

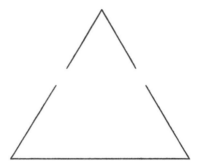

If you said a triangle, you are technically wrong. Actually it is two lines, one with one bend; the other with two bends. Your mind filled in the gap and created a triangle. This process is called visual closure.

There are many types of closure. Another example of visual closure is what your mind does when viewing film. Your mind provides the closure between a series of rapidly shown still photographs, creating the illusion of movement—moving pictures. Line drawings and cartoons require more closure than photographs. Artists who, with a few deft strokes of the pen, can capture the essence of a face or an object demand very high levels of closure, because the brain is forced into overdrive to mentally fill in what is missing.

In well-ordered music, closure is described as follows: The mind anticipates the next note, and when that note is the note the mind anticipated, the mind is, in effect, reinforced for making the right choice. For this reason, so-called modern music and also some kinds of oriental music—music based on principles of tonality different from our traditional music, and therefore unpredictable—are described as ugly, discordant, or twangy. Axioms such as "art is a function not of what you put in, but of what you leave out," and "less is more" testify to the artist's instinctive feel for the power of closure. At an everyday level, closure is what we call filling in the blanks, catching the drift, or jumping to conclusions.

Closure is the intellectual equivalent of the phrase "nature abhors a vacuum." The mind apparently abhors its own version of a vacuum—an enclosed series of ideas. Given discreet parts, the mind instinctively works to extract a meaning, create a whole. Indeed, it may be obsessed with—won't rest until—the whole is seen. And when the whole is seen, the result is delight. The brain is reinforced and gratified—delighted—with the results of its ability to close. This concept, *delight*, is, as we will see, one of the key objectives of a learning organization.

Adding Nine

The best example of closure in action is found in the inner workings of a joke. Assume a joke has 10 pieces of information. In other words, to get the joke you have to know all 10 pieces. The joke teller, instead of just giving you all 10 pieces, however, gives you 1 through 8, then 10—the punch line. Your job is to add nine.

$$1 \quad 2 \quad 3 \quad 4 \quad 5 \quad 6 \quad 7 \quad 8 \qquad 10$$
$$\uparrow$$
$$9$$

Mentally adding nine is known as getting it. If you can't add nine, you don't get it. Let's say a listener is not able to add the missing piece. What does the teller do? One thing the teller does not do, initially at least, is give it away. He or she will repeat the punch line, or repeat 7, 8, and 10, or retell the entire joke if necessary; then, only as a last resort, tell the person what nine is. And when the teller has to divulge nine, the joke isn't funny any more. If the teller accidentally lets it slip out while actually telling the joke, he or she might exclaim, "Oh no! I blew it!" The joke is ruined.

Why is this the case? Why is it so important that the hearers of the joke add the missing piece? Don't they get all 10 pieces of information either way? The answer is obviously that in a joke, discovery is the key. The delight results from adding the key piece yourself, not having to be told. To illustrate, take a look at the following joke.

> A 70-year-old man went in for a checkup. Impressed with the man's excellent physical condition, the doctor said: "You're in superb shape . . . strong heart, clear blood, good lungs . . . amazing. Tell me. How old was your father when he died?" "Who said he's dead?" replied the 70-year-old. "You mean he's alive?" asked the doctor. "Yessir," said the man. "He's 90 years old and we're going to play racquetball this afternoon." "Wow," said the doctor. "Well, then how old was your grandfather when he died?" "Who said he's dead?" said the 70-year-old. "Your grandfather is still alive?" marveled the doctor. "Yes, he's 112 years old and getting married next month." "Getting married," said the doctor, "that's amazing! But tell me, why would someone that old want to get married?" "Who said he *wanted* to?" replied the 70-year-old.

You're laughing. So, what was the missing nine? The grandfather had to get married, of course. But I didn't have to tell you. You added nine. You closed. Also, you closed with amazing speed. In a fraction of a second, in an instant, you added the missing piece.

At this point we can make a distinction between humor, which equates with closure, and funniness, which is primarily associated with content. Put another way, funniness is a function of the facts 1–10, whereas humor is a function of the process of adding 9. Even though this distinction may seem artificial, it is not wholly without basis.

In their original meaning, words such as humor and comedy (*comedia*) had less to do with funniness than with the idea of balance and the ultimate fitting-together of things. Which raises the question: If humor is equated with closure and separated from funniness, it is possible to have something which is humorous but not funny? The answer is yes.

In the film *Chinatown*, with Faye Dunaway and Jack Nicholson, there is a scene in which Nicholson is grilling Dunaway regarding the identity of a mysterious young girl who has been floating around throughout the picture. Dunaway won't answer, so Nicholson browbeats her. "Is she your sister? Is she your daughter? Your sister? Your daughter? Sister?! Daughter?!" he yells. "Yes!" Dunaway finally snaps.

The horrible truth is revealed. The girl is both her daughter and her sister. Faye is the victim of incest. Making matters worse is that the audience has met Faye's father. But now we know what he did—and we know it not because anybody told us but because we closed. Just as closure makes funny things funnier, it also makes horrible things more horrible. Faye's "Yes!" was the sobering punchline; an example of humor that wasn't funny.

At that point in the film, some people in the theatre did laugh. I saw the film a second time, and at the point of Faye's "Yes!," carefully observed the audience's reaction. There was an instant of silence. Then some people let out a low groan; others expelled a puff of air from their nose or mouth—a sort of shortened laugh; a few actually gave out with a brief laugh; a woman near me whispered "Oh, ish!" All of these reactions were the concrete indicators that closure had occurred. I daresay that the people who laughed did not do so because they thought it was funny. Their laugh was an involuntary expression of the terrible insight.

Equating humor and closure, and referring to things which are humorous but not funny should not cause too much confusion with the standard understanding of the word "humor." I stress it, however, in an attempt to pry the mechanism of humor loose from mere funniness without losing any of its power. In short, I want to take humor seriously, as a "delight"ful and integral engine of learning. In the broadest sense to be humorous is to require (and hope to produce) closure. Humor, in this sense, is the enabler of connections and insights, of what Piaget calls the experience of cognitive success associated with mastery and learning. It is the delight (whether the outcome is funny or tragic) of figuring out for yourself the fitting-togetherness of things.

Humor—or if you will, closure—is the mental process of making connections. It goes far beyond the practice of joke-telling. It applies to managing, selling, teaching, and parenting. In its broadest sense, closure is the mechanism of true inside-out learning. As a result, we can refine the definition of learning as follows:

Learning: Providing information and opportunities for closure.

The focus here is not on teaching. It does not focus on the outside-in activities of deciding what information people need and then giving it to them. Rather, the focus is on learning; on the inside-out process of gathering information and then deciding what to leave out so that nines will have to be added; so that insights will take place.

When people learn by closing—from the inside-out—the learning is more personal and it sticks longer. People not only get the point—they understand something. Their understanding transcends mere rational comprehension. Their minds and senses have been stimulated. They feel good. In short, they have been given something we all get precious little of, the chance to experience meaning, to feel understanding—closure.

The understanding and effective use of closure is one of the hallmarks of a learning organization. Particularly in a rapidly changing environment, it can be an effective tool for dealing with the known and coping with the unknown.

Dealing with the Unknown—Kronos, Kairos, and Chaos

Applying the ideas of kronos, kairos, and chaos in an organization involves the adoption of the chaos skill of looking for strange attractors. Specifically, it involves our being able to look at the random events of change not as a chaotic breaking up of the known, but as an emerging pattern that needs to be deciphered.

The ancient Greeks had two primary words for time. *Kronos*, the base for the English word chronology, is linear time. It also carries with it the implication of cause and effect. *Kairos* is best translated as the "right time": a point in time when all the pieces are in place and there is a potential for something to happen— provided somebody or something makes it happen. In the *New Testament*, for example, when Luke says, "Mary's time had come," he uses *kronos* because pregnancy was a predictable, linear process with a specific outcome. In the book of Matthew, when Christ says, "My time has not yet come," the word *kairos* is used because all the factors for Christ's passion are not yet in place. The time isn't right.

Another way to describe *kairos* is in terms of a window. When a *kairos*, or window, opens, there is a potential. This window may remain open indefinitely, or it may close. The window for a moon launch, for example, opens and closes depending on the moon's position, Florida's weather, and Congressional funding. The windows for certain inventions, however, open at some point in time and wait for someone to take advantage of them. Take the invention of the airplane. Some have stated that the window for the invention of the airplane opened when Leonardo da Vinci first sketched his plans for a flying machine. This is not true, however. Although the concept was present, the technology was not. The actual window for the airplane opened about 1890, give or take a few years, as a result of advances in steel production, petroleum refining, the invention of the internal combustion engine, and a rudimentary understanding of aerodynamics. In the 1890s, the technical and theoretical pieces existed for someone to put together and get the airplane off the ground. Even with all the pieces in place, it still took another 10 years for the Wright brothers to finally get a heavier-than-air craft to fly.

At the *kairos*, the right time, there is a potential for something to happen. In short, it is the opportunity for the proverbial idea whose time has come. In response to these windows I have observed three basic organizational reactions:

1. Ignore it: Keep on doing what we've been doing; work our strategy; regard the new set of affairs as an encumbrance to our *kronos* plan.

   I see many organizations working and reworking their strategies and plans to artificially extend a normative system—making real change only when forced to, and trying to solve all their problems quickly with new strategies and systems.

2. Test it: Focus on a pet idea or a goal and ask: "Is this the right time for _____ ?"

   One company had been thinking for a long time about moving from a distributor of other organizations' products to producing and selling its own products. They felt this was the best plan for the future and were continually feeling the pulse of their business environment waiting for the right time.

3. Explore it: Ask the question: "For what is this the *kairos*— the right time?"

These organizations are prepared to take radical departures. They are prepared to allow the environment to dictate to them (within reason) what their next direction or initiative should be.

To ignore it is, of course, the least productive response—unfortunately one that many organizations adopt. To test it is much better and often results in timely breakthroughs and advances. Both of these responses are rooted in the known. The first plants both feet in the past and refuses to move. The other plants one foot on solid ground and explores with other foot to find new solid ground.

The third response—explore it—is potentially the most productive but also the most risky. It requires both feet to float free, in search of new ground. It is not a blind leap, however. In terms of Woodward's First Law, the explore-it response is reacting to something rather than nothing. It looks at what may appear to others as a chaotic mass of unrelated things and asks "I wonder if there's anything here?" Or it responds to an intuition that says: "I think there's something new here." In all the disordered pieces, this response senses and searches for connections that will result in a whole. In short, the explore-it response wants to close on the disparate details and bring them into some kind of new order. It wants to make sense out of what appears to be nonsense.

Thus, one person's chaos is another person's *kairos*. The only difference between them is an attitude; the facts remain the same. One response recoils from chaos and retreats into the comfort of its *kronos*. The other response sees the seeming chaos for what it is—a *kairos*, a window opening. The mechanism for deciphering what that window represents is a function of applying closure techniques to recognize and specify ideas. The job of a learning organization is nothing less than to establish means and mechanisms to implement and support these techniques.

A changing organization presents a dizzying array of gaps, and a multitude of nines to fill them. The question is: Which one goes where? The most effective learning organizations, then, are those which can establish norms that foster inside-out thinking in order to activate and tie into the closure-making potential of their employees. The formulation of such norms finds its beginnings in the folds of the brain.

Playing to the Brain

The brain, we are told, is the most amazing organ in the body, able to coordinate a dazzling multiplicity of functions with speed and creativity. (Now we have to remember, of course, that this is the brain's opinion.) Our love affair with the brain is well founded but it sometimes allows us to overlook the fact that the brain is a tool like all the other organs, with its own set of characteristics. One of those characteristics, we have seen, is the ability to close. Another, related, characteristic is the tendency to generate options and solutions.

To begin probing this ability, I regularly ask groups, "How many of you are creative?" Some hands go up right away; some never go up; others vacillate. In general, the question is problematic because the word "creative" has a built-in value judgment. Creative is good. But since some people do not consider themselves creative—or assume creativity applies only to artistic people—they are forced to declare that they may lack something good, and are the lesser because of it. So then I say, "Well, since that question is problematic, let me ask another one: How many of you get ideas out of the blue?" The response is immediate, even startling. Backs straighten, eyes open, people nod, virtually all hands go up. Something has been struck. Creative or not, we all get ideas out of the blue.

Then I ask, "When—and where—do you get them?" The responses are always virtually the same. The most common are: in the car while driving; running; showering; brushing my teeth; ironing, or mowing the lawn (or while doing some other ordinary task); just before I fall asleep; while I'm sleeping; while I'm reading or watching TV; when I'm talking; or in a meeting.

Basically the categories are:

1. *Routine motor skills*—Driving, running, shaving, ironing, etc. When the mind is disengaged, and the muscles are performing on automatic, often coupled with a level of white noise (car engine, water running, etc.) which blots out other noises.

2. *Sleep*—Either in the twilight zone just before falling asleep or on waking up; or out of a dead sleep.
3. *Routine mental work*—Watching TV or reading; the brain can think faster than you can read or faster than people can talk; more often than not, the idea has nothing to do with what you are reading or listening to.
4. *Problem-solving sessions*—Discussion or meetings for the expressed purpose of generating ideas. (This example is always among the last mentioned and in the vast minority.)

The next question is, "What are these ideas about?" The answer is anything. They may be about important business matters or so-called trivial things. But they are about things that, as one person put it, are bugging you—things that are on your mind.

Finally I ask, "Did these ideas really come out of the blue? Out of nowhere?" The answer is no. The ideas are in response to questions or, more accurately, problems that have been put there, recently placed in the consciousness by circumstances. People often can't remember having consciously thought about the problem, but it was apparently there all along—being worked on. When the conscious mind is in neutral or otherwise occupied, the solutions pop out.

From this shared experience, we can draw some general conclusions:

- Problems, things we need resolved, no matter what they are, apparently go into our brains like solve commands into a computer: Once entered, the brain works tirelessly, day and night, to come up with a solution.
- The quality of the solution is commensurate with the quality of the information available.
- Our ability to receive our own solutions is apparently blocked by our conscious or competing thoughts; therefore the brain often has to wait until off times to communicate them to us.
- The reaction to these ideas popping out is initially one of delight.

To this list, I would add:

- The quality of the idea can vary and often needs interpretation and/or refinement.

Finally, I think it is important to note that those times when we are supposed to get ideas—when we're thinking about them, or in brainstorming or problem-solving meetings—are often the times when we are least likely to get them. To understand this point more fully, think of the following example. Most people have had the experience of seeing somebody they know but being unable to recall the person's name. In that situation, the harder you try to remember, the more blocked you become. And when do you remember the person's name? When they are gone, or the next day; in short, when the pressure is off. Similarly, often the harder we think about or try to come up with ideas and solutions, the more they evade us.

The lessons of these common phenomena are unfortunately all too often lost on organizations. The natural creative process is frequently frustrated by the need for quick results. A common scenario is one in which a group or a team meets to come up with responses to a current problem or need. They may just throw ideas around informally or they may draw on any one of a number of creativity, brainstorming, or systems-thinking techniques. But the pressure is on, and the focus is results—an idea, options, a solution. (As more organizations became familiar with more sophisticated and longer-term innovation techniques this knee-jerk response is diminishing; still, a large number of organizations have no in-place process for addressing one of their greatest needs—fostering experimentation.) They have needs but no norms. Thus, they are continually reacting—pushing—to come up with ideas quickly. The results are medium to low-grade ideas and little follow-up. What is needed is a process that is both simple and "brain friendly."

DATA DUMP, DOWNTIME, DRAW OUT

The 60s and 70s saw the rise in earnest of a number of creativity and innovation models to address the problem that, in response to emerging needs, organizations were continually jumping to solutions. Indeed, the term "solution-oriented thinking" became the specter that needed to be exorcised to enable progress. Actually, solution-oriented thinking was the simple expression of the normative mindset in which solutions were known and solutions could be formulated immediately. As the rate of change picked up and the need for original ideas increased, solution-oriented thinking did indeed need to be rooted out. The result was a proliferation of creativity models and techniques from creative brainstorming to synechtics to lateral thinking. The outcome of these methods was to generate alternative ideas: to get people out of their paradigms and categories; to see problems in new perspectives and generate and refine ideas to meet these problems.

The results were generally very positive. Now, instead of rushing into some hastily generated solution, organizations were taking time to step back and generate alternatives to widen their perspectives and their options. We have been refining and expanding these processes ever since.

The problem I find in the actual application of this method within organizations is that the creativity sessions are often once-and-for-all meetings in which groups are pressured to come up with a good alternative in that meeting. The result is often frustration and torpor. Groups hit the wall and grind down without really having produced a quality output. The situation is much the same as the situation mentioned earlier, when you see a person you know and can't recall the name. The harder you try, the less you are able to succeed. Therefore, I think it is necessary to build a little more into this process to make it less stressful and more brain friendly. More specifically, it is necessary, before trying to generate alternatives and ideas to prepare the brain in a focused but nonpressured way and then give the brain some time to work. The process is called Data Dump, Downtime, Draw Out. (Note: in presenting this method, I am fully aware that similar processes are part of many current creativity techniques; but I am also aware that in many organizations, the high-pressure brainstorming session is still the standard for creative idea generation.)

Data Dump

The data dump is a session or meeting designed to define or outline a problem and dump in all the data possible relating to that problem. The intent of this meeting is not to draw conclusions, come up with ideas, or go into any deep analysis. This process draws primarily on the basic rules of brainstorming and the methods of what is called "mindmapping" or "brainmapping." The steps in this stage are:

Define the problem. A problem is basically the difference between what you have and what you want. Quickly generate a "got vs. want" list—an accounting of what you have and what you need. If you can be explicit, good; if not, do what you can and move on. Describe your problem in a word or a phrase.

Create a "brain map." Write the word or phrase that describes the problem in the middle of a large sheet of paper or on a board. Then, observing the rules of brainstorming, generate as many facts as you can regarding the problem. (You can write these facts on the paper or board, or even better, use Post-it notes.) Facts include things that exist, things you know, people, statistics, feelings, hopes—in short, anything that has something to do with the problem. Keep going with this process until you run out of energy and facts. Normally it takes about 5 to 7 minutes, usually no more than 10.

Connect. Using pens or Magic Markers or highlighters, draw lines between things that are related or connected. Take some time to have each of the team members explain why they think certain facts are related or connected.

Program the brain. Based on the activities to this point, briefly restate or redefine the problem and then set a time a day or two later to reconvene to come up with ideas. Tell the team members that in the meantime their job is to come up with ideas and alternatives for addressing the problem. The data dump is designed to give the collective brains two things.

1. A clear definition of the problem.
2. A massive infusion of accurate and as-complete-as-possible information about that problem.

Since there is no pressure to solve, resolve, or conclude the problem or the process, this meeting is open. There is no expectation of success nor any fear of failure. If any ideas are offered they are recorded and held until later. The whole process should take less than an hour—more likely, closer to 45 minutes. The basic purpose of the process is to produce as much information as possible for the brain to begin to connect and close on.

Downtime

Downtime is simply an interval—ideally, one to two days after the information meeting—to allow the information to sink in and germinate. Group members are abandoned to their cars, their showers, their sleep, their reading, their day-dreaming—in short, to those places and times where they get ideas. During this time, only two rules need apply:

- *Expect an insight:* Condition yourself to expect ideas, hunches, plans, feelings, etc. They will begin to appear.
- *Record your results:* Establish some method—usually a note pad or a small tape recorder—to capture your ideas and insights. (This process is often the most difficult for reasons of inconvenience and lack of alertness. It is difficult to record ideas when you are driving, showering, or running; it is also difficult to record things when you are relaxed or semi-awake.)

Draw Out

We have now come full circle. We have arrived at the point where many creativity methods begin—the idea-generating step. The draw out stage is the time for generating ideas and evaluating options. In the next chapter we will call this the "Creative Problem Solving Meeting." As mentioned earlier, the number of models and methods to promote creativity and generate ideas could (and does!) fill a multitude of books and tapes and seminars. The key steps in this final stage are:

- *Develop ideas and options.* Use any of the numerous methods available.
- *Evaluate your output.* On a 1 to 10 scale, evaluate your final outputs. If they don't score in the 8 to 10 range, you might

want to consider repeating the draw out stage or perhaps even repeat data dump.

CONCLUSION

In this chapter, we have traveled from the sublime to (in the best sense of the word) the mundane. We begin with discussions of creativity, closure, *kairos,* and learning organizations and concluded with a process—a norm—for conveniently and effectively generating ideas and options. The basic points of this chapter are:

- To survive, changing organizations will have to rely more and more on their ability to be creative and innovative.
- Outmoded systems in organizations will not be replaced suddenly with new systems; rather they will be replaced with ideas that grow into new systems.
- Changing organizations therefore need an in-place method to value ideas and build specificity.
- The human brain, when given the opportunity, has a tremendous desire and capacity to close—to make connections and fill in gaps to create new concepts and ideas.
- Many current organizational creativity and idea-generating methods (if they even have any methods) focus on generating options quickly and thus put pressure on people to produce on cue.
- It is more productive (and brain friendly) to allow people to define facts, explore connections, and mentally process (off line) before expecting them to produce results.
- It is important (and fairly easy) to establish efficient norms for creative problem solving in organizations by dividing the process into the stages of data dump, downtime, and draw out.

Once implemented, this process avoids the often self-defeating pressure to produce on demand and offers an alternative to the often complex demands of some creativity methods. Finally, it capitalizes on the inherent strengths of the inside-out, closure-producing potential of the brain.

What organizations in change need today is *not* another creativity method but, instead, the normalization of a process to generate and refine ideas on an ongoing/as-needed basis. The simpler and less time-consuming this process, the more likely it will be used. In this chapter, we have introduced such a process—one that operates with its own logic and purpose but is able to incorporate already existing creativity techniques and methods. Such a simple method can become the engine of a successfully experimenting learning organization.

Chapter Seven

Navigating through Change

There is even a Catch-22 to catching up: when you get there, 'there' isn't there anymore.

Stanley M. Davis
Future Perfect

The only way to change is to change—sort of like having a drink to get over a hangover.

William Bridges

F undamentally, an organization in change is like any other organization. It needs to set goals, develop strategies, establish
rewards, and provide feedback and support. An organization in
change, however, differs in two respects: First, it needs to do certain things *before* it attends to its traditional functions; second,
those traditional functions often require fundamentally different
methods to succeed in the chaotic environment. We have identified two key before-change elements, (1) developing personal
openness and (2) providing support to help others address loss,
establish trust, and in general, translate enough anxiety into fear
to generate some measure of focused action. The key skill of communication can then help the organization bridge from minus
one to plus one. In chapters 3, 4, and 5, we saw how the traditional words—openness, communication, and support—took on
a new meaning and focus appropriate to change. Finally our discussion of the learning organization has put us squarely in the
plus-one area of experimentation. The purpose of this chapter is
to complete the key elements of the plus-one side, specifically,
the crucial aspects of strategy development and team process
necessary to support the ongoing needs of a fluid and evolving
organization.

GOALS VERSUS OUTCOMES: STRATEGY REDEFINED

What the world needs least is another goal-setting model. Those
of us who have had to submit weekly, monthly, or quarterly objectives—especially if we are refugees from some legalistic management by objectives (MBO) system—we've had quite enough
of that. But just saying it won't make it go away. While setting
goals may be a necessary evil, establishing a direction and formulating a strategy are survival skills. So the question becomes:
In a changing environment, what does a strategy look like and
how is it set?

"In principle," writes Stanley Davis, "strategy precedes organization."[1] It makes perfect sense to proceed from strategy to action; you have to know where you are going before you can develop a plan to get there. But as Davis asserts, typically strategy

is nothing more than "the codification of what has already taken place," and increasingly, organizations based on this model "are created for businesses that either no longer exist or are in the process of going out of existence!"[2] Perhaps he overstates his case, but maybe not. A friend of mine who recently left IBM told me that when he worked there in the 80s, the best managers were the number crunchers. "We owned the world, we could set goals—and meet them! It was all a matter of good forecasting and planning." Strategy was the application of a known system. ("This is no longer true," he added.)

In a chaotic environment the power of prediction is lost. Even with prodigious amounts of information (and the amounts would have to be prodigious as well as prophetic) the best you could expect is to break even—to catch up with the present. And, as Davis observes "there is even a Catch-22 to catching up: When you get there, 'there' isn't there anymore."[3]

So, in the final analysis, planning and strategy are more a matter of what Davis terms *interpolation* than of extrapolation.[4] Beyond simply exhorting people to work smarter or telling them that our new rule is "ready, fire, aim," what are some practical ways to develop a strategy? I have found two methods that can form the basis for a resilient planning process—changing verbs to nouns and working backward to move forward.

VERBS TO NOUNS

I often ask groups to write down one or two departmental outcomes they want to accomplish. I stay away from goal and objective and let them define outcome any way they wish. Because they are generally scrambling to cope with a host of changes, they don't have any difficulty identifying desired outcomes. Then I ask them to get in groups of three or four and compare their outcomes and decide if they are nouns or verbs. After a brief discussion on what is a noun versus a verb, they classify their outcomes. Thus far we are running about 80 percent verbs, 20 percent nouns.

These percentages are not surprising, given the fact that people are generally taught to think about goals in verb forms: "To implement . . . ," "To complete . . . ," etc. Verbs express action, activity, and direction I am told. Because of their action bias, verb seems like the right answer. As the groups report in, I often see people whose outcomes came out as nouns quickly trying—with a few pen strokes—to make them into verbs. But nouns are okay too. They define end states: "An in-place, functioning network of . . . ," "$10,000.00 in sales of . . . ." Actually, both the verbs and the nouns in their examples tend to have that MBO how-much-of-what-by-when feel to them. Obviously we have all been well trained.

Then I break the news to them. In a changing environment, nouns are actually more functional than verbs. A cheer goes up. Deep down, it seems, they have hated those verbs all along. Thinking of goals as verbs is a functional attitude in a stable, closed-box environment. They define activities. They tend to select out and stipulate established practices and procedures for known outcomes. "Implement," "finalize," "establish." They tend not to define the how because the what is a given or a known. People know how (or better, there is a procedure) to accomplish their objective. But what if the how and the what aren't known? Then you're better off with a noun.

To illustrate this idea, let me present a very basic example. I once worked with a discount retail store similar to Kmart and Wal-Mart. The store was undergoing tremendous change due to competition and new marketing trends. They were scrambling, and one of their strategies was to increase the number of sales and specials on selected items to draw people into the store. The trouble was, people were showing up at some stores with newspaper clippings of sale items but then couldn't find the item or get the correct sale price. Obviously, some things were falling between the cracks. The head office, it seems, would put ads in the papers but somehow fail to tell all the stores and/or supply them with stock. This was clearly a change-related problem. So I asked them: What outcome do you want? They wrote the following:

"To enable customers to locate and purchase correctly-priced sale items."

Their MBO instructor would have been proud. It may have lacked a time/quantity element (how much by when) but for a first cut it wasn't bad. But it was a verb. What does enable mean? I asked. Blank stares. Enable was an empty word. No matter how much they quantified and specified, the word enable would continue to beg definition. So, I asked, if you enabled this outcome, what would exist?

"Exist?"

"Yes, what would exist? What would be in place?"

So the data dump started. It began with a smiley face—a satisfied customer standing at the cash register with his or her toaster in hand getting the correct price. That was the end state. The other things that would have to exist to enable this outcome were:

- Signs directing people to the toasters.
- A correct price programmed into the computer.
- Stock in the back room (the store warehouse).
- Stock on the shelves.
- Extra staff on sale days.

And since a main part of the problem was a communication breakdown at the main office, they added:

- Timely information regarding upcoming sales.
- A computer program that directed the main warehouse to send stock to the stores on time.

Now they could act. They could go the verb route and assign specific tasks to specific people, put up signs, program the computer, check with the main office. Although this example is a basic one, its principle can apply to more complex situations in which solutions and approaches need to evolve. The power of what I call a noun—a concrete but as yet unfinished or nonexistent thing— is to focus creative action. It functions in the same ways as the nine mentioned in Chapter 6. It demands resolution—closure. Simple as this sounds, it amazes me how organizations still get caught up in the unfocused action-orientation of verb, or activity, thinking.

The noun here is not the carefully crafted noun phrase of the normative goal-setting techniques. Rather, it is a list, a roughed

out, ongoing list of things—people, procedures, programs—
that needs to be in place to accomplish the outcome. The key is
concreteness.

The first step then in developing a strategy is simple. (If the
verb/noun distinction seems cumbersome or artificial, let it go.)
The point is to get people thinking about what they want or need
(their outcomes) in terms of concrete things that need to be in
place; and (not trying to be complete or thorough at first) simply
generate enough information to get a start. The details will fall in
place as the chaotic system evolves.

When I ask people to take the one- or two-sentence outcome
statements they have generated and make a list of things needed
to achieve this outcome and then to explain their list to one other
person, they are surprised how much better they understand
what their jobs really are and where they are going. The mere act
of definition, it seems, gets their cognitive, closure-producing
gears rolling, initiating a fledgling strategy-producing action
which seems to take on a life of its own.

"What about the details? The particulars?" As mentioned earlier, the world does not need another goal-setting model. In the
spirit of the focus on introducing practical applications of more
complex change concepts, suffice it to say that managers and
leaders will be well served taking a short period of quality time to
define their outcomes in terms of concrete elements that need
to be in place. But in another sense, we need to continue this
discussion by asking: Once you develop such a list, what have
you really got? The answer is a working hypothesis, not a plan.
This is a key distinction: As managers and leaders we must learn
to establish concrete outcomes that will act as catalysts rather
than solutions.

WORKING BACKWARD, MOVING FORWARD

Flying from New York to Kansas City is an in-box operation. It
relies on careful up-front planning (the flight plan) and possible
mid-course corrections along the way. It also relies on the fact
that Kansas City is where you want to go and further, that Kansas
City will not move before you get there. This model—the pilot

model—is the standard for traditional, normative planning. Traveling by wagon train from Kansas City to California in the 1840s is another model altogether. It relies on a compelling vision or goal—a new life, free land, riches. It also presents a basic direction—west. Along the way, however, it is necessary to continually send out scouts to check rivers, passes, water holes, potential hostilities. Following the scouts' advice, the wagon train makes adjustments, changes course, backtracks, or even turns back altogether. If they happen to meet someone from California, the pioneers want to know, is there still land? Where? Gold? Is it worth it? How about Oregon? Based on feedback, the wagon train can change not only its direction but also its destination, or even its purpose. In spite of this flexibility, on a day-to-day basis the wagon train has a solid grounding in what it's doing and where it's going. This model—the scout model—is more appropriate to a changing environment.

Consequently, to move forward we have to work backward from proposed outcomes. We have to send out feelers and ideas in the direction of what we currently see as our future objectives—try things out, experiment—and then reevaluate our progress on the information coming back, continually updating our strategy to correspond to the shifting reality. As a result we are always connected with our future and grounded in our present. There are a number of expressions of this point of view—from the purely theoretical to the more practical calls for bottom up management and listening to the guy on the shop floor. These all recognize the same basic principle: Whereas in a racing shell the captain tells the crew what to do, in a rubber raft the crew and the captain take responsibility for direction and strategy.

More specifically, organizations and people in white water have to shed the pilot model; have to discard the heavy up-front commitment of time to develop a plan that is simply followed. Rather, they will be better served if they develop an efficient process to define outcomes and generate options which can be revisited and revised on an ongoing basis.

We can now see how the operational pieces of change management begin to fit together. In response to change, organizations need to move away from a plan/control/monitor mindset to an observe/communicate/experiment point of view. Specifically, they need to establish norms for fostering and valuing ideas as well as engage in producing an ongoing and constantly updated list of nouns—for working backward to move forward. There is no shortage of systems and ideas to accomplish this integration, but a template I have found both practical and useful is as follows:

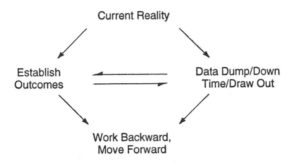

1. **Establish current reality.** Using the communication tool presented in Chapter 4, establish an intellectual and emotional baseline for meeting the demands of current changes.
2. **Establish outcomes.** Possibly as part of establishing current reality but more likely as an extension of it, set aside a dedicated period of time to define outcomes (objectives or goals) and the things that need to be in place:
   a. *Identify outcomes*—Gain clarity and consensus regarding general outcomes (desired end states).
   b. *Solicit ideas*—Generate ideas and options for achieving these outcomes.
   c. *Identify nouns*—Generate a list of things that need to exist or be in place to accomplish the outcome.

This process need not be lengthy or involved. Its purpose is to define a clear direction and develop a first-cut list of outcomes. If the outcomes are not clear or if there is disagreement or confusion about them, then you may need to move into a creative problem-solving mode (data dump/downtime/draw out) to clarify or define them. Or, as the model also indicates, you may proceed directly from the current reality meeting to the creative problem-solving meeting. In either case you will need to establish a set of concrete outcomes before moving forward to the final stage, work backward, move forward:

3. **Work backward, move forward.** This stage is the trying out and testing of your plans in the spirit of the scout model. You will then begin to alter and add to your outcome list, based on the feedback you get in the process of implementation.

   This process is not so much meeting-heavy as it is punctuated with time-outs. Although it seems (from a normative point of view) like a stutter-stop approach, it is, in practice, the kind of approach that in terms of efficiency and results is best suited to a rapidly changing environment. The process is relatively straightforward; the key is discipline and breaking old habits.

My first job was teaching college English. My first big insight in that job was that I couldn't really teach students to write. But I could teach them to organize, and once they were organized, their writing improved markedly. The obstacle I had to overcome in teaching them to organize, however, was their conception of an outline. They all had what I like to call the "Miss Furd" concept of an outline. Miss Furd is the archetypal old-school English teacher who made them write outlines before they started their papers, and enforced the legalistic rules of outlining (every A must have a B and every 1, a 2, etc.) In short, she advocated the pilot model. Most students, however, were not writing about a subject as much as they were exploring that subject. So I helped them develop a scout version of outlining—quick, flexible, repeatable, and evolving. "Don't spend any more than 5 to 10 minutes," I told them. Go as far as you can with the main points and support. Write against those points. When the outline breaks down or calls for a deeper cut, stop, and flesh out a new outline. And so on. Finally, the outline became for them a tool, not a burden.

The process here is the same. The methods introduced take advantage of the best theory to provide a flexible, repeatable set of skills with the hope of providing some nouns for managing chaotic change on a day-to-day basis.

As you can see, to support this whole process, managers would be well served by a large number of supporting skills in the areas of group process, creativity, planning, consensus building, and negotiation. Indeed, the better you handle the change issues up front the more appropriate some of the more traditional management skills become. It is not our intent to re-invent any of these wheels. Our focus has been on bringing into high relief some of the essential distinctions between stable and changing environments and then to provide simple (but not sim-plistic) techniques that can actually be used. How you use it will depend on your needs, your people, your background, and your time limits. The template is there.

Before going on to the final discussion—positive contention—there are two points that need to be made regarding intuition and confidence.

A NOTE ON INTUITION

It is widely recognized that in a chaotic environment, intuition rises in importance. This evaluation inevitably receives mixed re-actions. Some react positively because it allows people and orga-nizations to free themselves of the manacles of rigid, logical thinking and planning; others react negatively, claiming that free-dom from systematic approaches will only foster sloppy thinking and reliance on unreliable hunches. These polarized views grow out of the common assumption that intuition is an exclusively right-brained, creative, and soft phenomenon without any kind of rigor or responsibility. This point of view is erroneous. Intu-ition is better understood in terms of pattern recognition.

In neurological terms (an acquaintance once explained to me) things that are known to us are located at certain points, or run along certain paths, in the brain. Theoretically we could take a penlight, he went on, and highlight the point, or trace the path and say, "There. That's where that knowledge or habit resides." Intuition, however, deals with things that the brain does not yet know but has some or all of the information to figure it out. In-stead of a penlight, intuition is more like a flashlight. We shine it on a certain area of the brain and say, "It's in there somewhere. Look carefully. Figure it out." Thus the hunch, or feeling, or nag-ging sense of a connection is not without basis.[5] The brain is trying to close; it is working to add enough nines to make a whole. The resulting insight may take the form of a hunch, a feeling, an idea, a list or a full-blown plan. But whatever form it takes, it is—at the point of inception—still a working hypothesis that needs to be tried out and checked out.

Although this progression is the brain's natural way of processing new information, the process itself has often been devalued in favor of more analytical and hard methods. As a result, the current activity around developing new methods to manage change is helping us remember something we already know—that the ostensibly soft notion of intuition has a steel core running through it.

Thus, a reliance on intuitive strategy is a hallmark of a changing organization. Intuitive strategy is a logical and conscious process, not a last resort. If you have provided yourself with concrete outcomes, you can work backward from them and enable yourself to then move forward, as Davis puts it, "so that implementing actions seems to flow intuitively from their recognition."[6] These actions are not being implemented, as much as they are being tested. Thus the process as a whole is an iterative, looping one which must always allow time for evaluation and alteration. Intuition, finally, is not a will-o-the-wisp but a workhorse. Its primary difference from traditional strategy planning is that rather than proceeding from its conclusions, it arrives at them—and then moves on.

A COMMENT ON CONFIDENCE

"But I have to demonstrate confidence. My people need that." I hear this comment over and over—and I agree with it. Managers and leaders in a chaotic environment need to demonstrate confidence: not a chauvinistic confidence in their ability to overcome all odds, but a more resilient confidence in their ability to figure things out. However, with this expression of confidence often comes the invisible rider of certainty—and that's where the problem lies.

In her wonderful book *Mindfulness*, psychologist Ellen Langer writes:

If a manager is confident but uncertain—confident that the job will get done without being certain of exactly the best way of doing it—employees are likely to have more room to be creative, alert, and self-starting.[7]

Confident but uncertain? It seems to fly in the face of good management. Stable organizations value confidence and certainty. Indeed, their confidence is a function of their certainty—their demonstration that they have everything under control. As a result, managers tend to:

- Know the system.
- Feign knowledge.
- Have the answers.

- Evaluate suggestions.
- Avoid risks.
- Be in charge.

In response, employees tend to:

- Follow procedures.
- Hide mistakes.
- Withhold suggestions.

- Go around the system.
- Defer to position.
- Wait for orders.

Changing organizations need to develop new attitudes toward uncertainty and new forms of confidence. Increasingly, managers will have to admit that they are uncertain (which everyone already knows) and generate confidence, not in their ability to solve problems, but in the team's or the department's ability to collaboratively generate options.

When this happens, managers will:

- Admit what they don't know.
- Publicize mistakes.
- Solicit suggestions.

- Collaboratively develop systems.
- Implement and evaluate approaches.

In response, employees will:

- Be self-starting.
- Take more risks.
- Feel better and more in control.

- Be more alert to problems/opportunities.
- Offer suggestions and options.

Ultimately a confident but uncertain approach takes the risk out of risk taking.

This call for confidence with uncertainty is, I find, a point that needs not so much to be argued as simply mentioned. Once aware of the distinctions, people often tend to realize that their confidence has been tinged with certainty; and having realized this fact, they are often relieved and more than willing to jettison it. For others, it is more difficult to part with. Without a conscious measure of studied uncertainty, however, change managers will sabotage their own efforts.

POSITIVE CONTENTION

The confrontation all started during a much-needed discussion of how to shorten the design process—how to reduce the time between the client's request for a tailored system and the implementation of that system. It soon became a heated discussion with two contending points of view. As both of what had become sides marshaled their evidence, the debate became more pointed, and caustic. It was about to lapse into personal innuendo, and even attack, when the manager stepped in.

His intervention was at first a violation of the rules of the meeting which had been billed as a team problem-solving session in which everybody was equal. His now assuming a boss role met with tacit resistance. "I thought this was supposed to be like King Arthur's round table—so no one can sit at its head!" someone mentioned. "Well, that was Arthur's intent," the manager joked, "but we have to remember that, at his round table, Arthur still had the biggest chair." Nobody laughed.

His humor was lost on the group, the manager assumed, because of the tension inherent in the discussion. Without giving it a second thought, he proceeded to, what he later called, "bring the two sides together" by pointing out that at one level they "really weren't in disagreement at all" and, further, that the differences in opinion regarding the timing and techniques "could certainly be worked out." The meeting ended with a seeming consensus regarding some next steps and what appeared to be agreement between the two contending points of view.

Nothing could have been further from the truth. The manager, it is true, left the meeting with a sense of having avoided conflict and facilitated problem solving. The other members of the team, however, went away with a strong sense of frustration—even anger. Their point of view was: we weren't heard; the issues, much less any options, were not clarified; the so-called solution was useless; and that nothing had been accomplished other than getting further behind. The meeting was a typical example of conciliation over collaboration.

In any organizational environment, but particularly in a changing environment, there is—and should be—a continual flow of contending sides. The creative process not only breeds but relies for its quality, on different points of view. Some Japanese companies, for example, hire mid-career managers from other organizations to help create alternative cultures and thus actually encourage contention. In his call for a new mindset for problem solving, Ralph Stacey advocates "Learning groups of managers—working in spontaneously self-organizing networks—that encourage open conflict . . . and publicly test assertions."[8] In short, there is ample support for the idea that conflict is not only good but essential for positive change. What I have found, however, is that the methods to manage this process often lag behind the needs of the process.

Typically, when groups or teams form they proceed from membership to subgrouping to confrontation.[9] Membership refers to

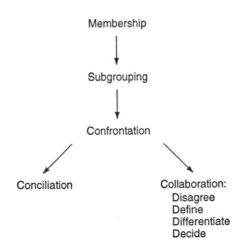

the initial stages in the process when problems and issues are discussed and points of view or opinions begin to emerge. Subgrouping refers to the forming of factions, points of view, or sides. Confrontation refers to the interaction when two or more subgroups come into contact with each other, take positions, and become protective or defensive. At this point, the group or team can go in one of two directions: conciliation or collaboration. The conciliation route seeks to reduce tension and resolve differences as quickly as possible. The collaboration route seeks to sustain and even increase the conflict for the purposes of clearer definition and problem solving.

By their nature, organizations—more specifically, managers—want to take the conciliation path. The reasons for this often implicit choice are well documented, oftentimes characterized as the phenomenon of heroic management.[10] This tendency is bred of a stable system's aversion to true conflict. It is based on ingrained normative rules such as: conflict is nonproductive; managers need to be in charge; people shouldn't have to fight; solutions can be settled through rational discourse; and a little disagreement is healthy but conflict means were out of control.

In a changing environment, I have found that:

1. The demand for innovative responses and the necessity to implement what are often half-baked solutions cause tension and a sense of being out of control.

2. This tension often results in disagreement and conflict that go beyond the unwritten rules of proper corporate behavior, and appear to be destructive.

3. Managers and leaders recoil in the face of this conflict and try heroic means to reduce tension and promote compromise.

4. These efforts only frustrate the process and suppress the issues.

As a result, when I suggest that managers really ought to encourage conflict in these situations—bait discord and sustain open disagreement—I run into some of the strongest reactions I experience in my work. Theirs is not a response of disagreement, but of discomfort and confusion. It is axiomatic that conflict can be healthy and that sweeping things under the rug is unhealthy, but as one manager put it, "Just mediating this conflict, much less actually encouraging it—on top of the fact that everybody is stressed out already—you've got to be kidding! Why don't I just put a gun in my mouth and pull the trigger?"

An overreaction? Not really. The words are exaggerated but the spirit is not. People and managers have enough trouble already. They don't need more. What they need is a way to somehow contend positively, to encourage disagreement in a way that focuses on the problem and the process, not the people.

To conclude the book, I offer a process which gives substance to the collaboration arm of the diagram on page 182. More to the point, it is a positive contention method (in chaos terminology, one characterized by bounded instability) to enable groups, departments, and teams to disagree, define, differentiate, and decide.

The success of this process is dependent on a group leader or facilitator recognizing the intellectual and emotional needs of people at each step, and meeting those needs before proceeding to the next step.

1. **Disagree**—Once sides or points of view emerge in a group, disagreement follows naturally. Exponents generally express their points of view minimally at first. They pull their punches, often employing irony and innuendo. Only later does this jabbing erupt into open, hostile conflict. The job of the leader is to recognize when this disagreement starts, and guide it. The basic skills are:

    Encourage: Encourage individuals to express their opinions.

    Amplify: Push them to express opinions with prompts like: "What else?" "Is that all?" "Can you clarify . . . or expand?" and "I feel there is more." Also you can actually "bait" disagreement with phrases such as "Your view appears quite different from" or "What is it about their argument that you don't like?"

    Guard: Allow only one person to speak at a time without interruption or rejoinder. Let the person speaking have the stage and guard his or her right to maintain it.

The disagree stage is clearly the least comfortable stage in the process. Once the guidelines are established, however, people will respect them—*Intellectually:* This stage enables people to begin understanding each other; *Emotionally:* This stage allows people to fully express themselves.

2. **Define**—Once views have been expressed, it is necessary to summarize or recap them. Make this stage as brief but as clear as possible:

Summarize:	The leader or other designated person formally summarizes the points of view to the satisfaction of the proponents of that view.
Record:	Record the point of view in writing— on paper or flip chart.

The define stage brings clarity to the contending issues—*Intellectually:* This stage provides a clear understanding of the opinions or viewpoints; *Emotionally:* People feel "heard"; they can say, "Yes, you understand me." This sense of being heard is essential; it legitimizes my point of view, whether people agree with it or not. As a result, the combative or defensive urge inherent in conflict is greatly diminished or reduced. We can see our disagreement—stripped of its emotional armor—for what it really is.

3. **Differentiate**—We have now gotten by what would otherwise be an emotional impasse (that probably would have resulted in dysfunctional behavior) and can engage in more traditional forms of problem solving. To differentiate is simply to formally compare and contrast the points of view. Even though this process will be working with the same facts as before, the fact that everybody has had the chance to be heard has allowed them to perceive the issues as information to be considered rather than positions to be defended or attacked. The general steps in this stage are:

Clarify the purpose:	Clarify (or more likely re-clarify) the original purpose of the problem-solving session; what is its desired outcome; its goal?
Weigh the options:	Allow each subgroup to explain its point of view, weighing its idea or solution against the purpose.
Cross-examine:	Allow the other group(s) to question the options being presented.

The Differentiate stage is the beginning of the more traditional decision-making process—*Intellectually:* This stage allows the groups to define and clarify the differences between their points of view vis-à-vis the purpose or goal. The result is an open, honest examination of the critical differences between the options; *Emotionally:* People feel in control and also responsible to the overall purpose of the team. In addition, instead of critical or protective behavior, they will more likely begin to see supportive behavior as well as the emergence of creative alternatives.

   4. **Decide**—To decide is simply to select one of the options or come up with a new option:

Present options:	Lay out the contending options and/or any new options.
Revisit the purpose:	Briefly remind everybody of the purpose or goal.
Decide by consensus:	By consensus vote or discussion, select an option.

Intellectually: People feel that the decision has been made fairly with respect to the purpose; *Emotionally:* Even if they don't totally agree with the outcome, people feel that they were heard and that the final solution was not forced on anyone.

In all, the collaboration route of disagree, define, differentiate, and decide allows the flame of conflict to temper the process so that people's points of view are heard and examined, and a fair decision is made. Clearly the key step in this process is the disagree step. To encourage, to actually bait contention flies in the face of many organizational norms and personal comfort levels. This kind of disagreement is essential (and also very efficient) in the process of identifying and evaluating options. Positive contention is, in short, a chaos skill, designed to identify strange attractors, quantify options, and establish a direction.

CONCLUSION—GOOD NEWS AND BAD NEWS

The tools of positive contention, as well as the other tools in this book particularly the techniques of support, have some good news and some bad news.

The good news is that the skills are simple and they work.
The bad news is that they only work with normal people.

"Well, that lets us out," you may be thinking. But before you draw any conclusions, consider that by normal I mean, simply, people who are willing to play fair. Specifically, they are the people who, when presented with a process or a method, are willing to give it the benefit of the doubt, submit to its stages or requirements, and try it out.

Abnormal people are those who do not seem to respond to the so-called rules of fair play—the people who stay angry no matter what you do, who refuse to budge on an issue because of the principle of the thing, who refuse to give any ground on their position, or who just plain won't take a chance. As we have seen in our discussions of stated and real goals, reactions to change, and positive contention, there are often reasons—not excuses, necessarily—but reasons for these responses. Sometimes their abnormality is justified; mostly it is not.

So, people in the world of organizational change can be divided into normal and abnormal—those who play fair and those who don't. There are more who are normal than abnormal, although the ratio varies from place to place. One thing I have found, however, is that most of the time when so-called abnormal people are treated normally—that is, they are given a plan or tool for dealing with their issues—they suddenly become quite normal.

Drawing on the water motif one final time, an abnormal response reminds me of something my water safety instructor told us in college (and which I later had the opportunity to experience firsthand): "Drowning people aren't particularly reasonable," he said "When you approach them, they're likely to react in a way that's dangerous to the both of you. But if you can somehow communicate that you know what you're doing and that there's some skill being applied, they get cooperative real quick."

People in change are much the same. They're looking for help and direction. If you can present those, they'll likely become cooperative and go with it.

Conclusion

Dreams of Wakefulness

For most people, change means keeping things the same, only better.

Tom Fosse

Managers involved in change who aren't scared are dangerous.

Daryl Conner

I n college I had the problem of falling asleep in class and dreaming I was awake. I would drag into the classroom exhausted from a late night of studying, and soon drift off. In my slumber, I dreamt I was in the same classroom, alert and refreshed, tracking with the lecture, taking good notes, experiencing a profound sense of learning at a deep level.

Meanwhile, in the real classroom, my fitful slumber became the object of curiosity and amusement. Other students watched as my head dropped back, caught itself, and came slowly forward. This nodding continued until the inevitable big one—the one where the head drops all the way back and hits the chair, followed immediately by a convulsive jerk as the eyes click open, only to gaze in horror at the gallery of onlookers, not to mention seeing that my pen had long since fallen from my fingers and was lying on the floor.

What followed then was (for me, at least) grim catch-up. Attempting to reestablish some measure of dignity, I retrieved my pen and began to take notes. I tried to pick up the thread of the lecture by remembering the dream, only to realize that the lecture in my dream had nothing to do with the one in class.

Many may have had the experience of falling asleep in a lecture, perhaps even dreaming they were awake, but certainly of being disoriented and confused on waking up. This shared experience helps us begin to understand what is happening on a larger scale with people and organizations today.

Tom Peters observes that after World War II the American economic climate was so favorable that success was virtually assured. Great strides were made; new management practices implemented. The problem, Peters notes, is that organizations drew the inevitable but erroneous conclusion that there was a cause-and-effect relationship between the practices and the success. On the contrary, he contends, there was no such relationship. The climate was so favorable that corporations succeeded sometimes even in *spite* of their management practices.

One might argue then that during that time, the corporate and educational establishment fell asleep and began to dream it was awake. During the 50s there were some fits and starts in the form of Sputnik and mild recessions, but it wasn't until the 60s and 70s that increased international influence and domestic smugness began to cause the big drops and convulsive jerks of waking up. The struggle continues. We are still in the waking process.

In my own work I see many organizations fighting the persistent and, for them, annoying demands of wakefulness. The key words they mumble in their restless, half-awake state are systems and control and normal. The sense of normalcy and relative comfort they experienced in the past tells them that if they just develop *new* systems—to bring things under control—they will experience a similar sense of normalcy in the future. They preach creativity and risk, but the manacles of maintenance behavior prevent them from becoming too creative or too risky. At its primary level, then, change is not just a concept or an incident but a nagging reality—an alarm clock that won't stop ringing. Organizations can choose to deal with it or they can turn over, pull the corporate covers over their heads and lapse into their dreams of wakefulness.

The trick is getting people and organizations to face that reality.

One of the greatest obstacles to that recognition is a sense of helplessness; the feeling that we can't do anything about it. A friend who is a physician tells me, not surprisingly, that with most diseases there is some denial, but that denial is always greater with those diseases for which there is no ready or easy cure. Similarly, organizations hesitate to admit that they have crossed the line—that their box has been broken—for fear of being cut adrift without a solution. Or that the solution will be so complicated or involved that it won't be worth it. And to be sure, the list of approaches and solutions to deal with change is long and complex. Thus, more than another approach, people need a place to start: a foothold.

In these pages I have tried to offer not a solution but a direction. They present not a comprehensive program but a set of basics—key skills and techniques for establishing a fluid strategy to establish and manage a change culture. This strategy begins on the inside and moves out. It stresses the need for people to understand their own reactions and become more open; and then to support others by helping them fully understand and verbalize their own reactions. With these emotional issues exposed and legitimized, the organization can move into a chaotic culture with a firmer sense of how and when to communicate and, finally, how to work together to experiment and test out new ideas.

Chaos, as we have seen, may be a word whose time has finally come. From a generic term for disorder and fear, it is now taking on the sense of underlying order and direction. But, if not the word itself, certainly our understanding of change has progressed from the ominous predictions of future shock and its accompanying denials to a more realistic assessment that we're in it for the duration and that we are going to need new skills and mindsets to make it through. This realization will, we hope, enable us to see patterns in the seeming variability of events and thus provide our organizations and our people with the robustness they need to cope with changes.

As the process of change continues, and a track record begins to emerge, there will undoubtedly be new approaches and solutions of greater clarity and simplicity. But that, to loosely quote Dostoevski, is the subject of a new book; our present book is finished.

Notes

Preface

1. Peter F Drucker, *Post-Capitalist Society* (New York: Harper Business, 1993), p. 59.
2. Ralph D Stacey, *Managing the Unknowable* (San Francisco: Jossey-Bass, 1992), p. 1.

Chapter One

1. George A Land, *Grow or Die: The Unifying Principle of Transformation* (New York: John Wiley & Sons, 1973; Buffalo, NY: Creative Education Foundation, 1992).
2. George Land and Beth Jarman, *Breakpoint and Beyond: Mastering the Future—Today* (New York: Harper Business, 1992).
3. Robert H Wiebe, *The Search for Order 1877–1920* (New York: Hill and Wang, 1967).
4. Charles Handy, *The Age of Unreason* (Boston: Harvard Business School Press, 1989), p. 5.
5. James Gleick, *Chaos: Making a New Science* (New York: Penguin Books, 1987), p. 5.
6. Stacey, *Managing the Unknowable*, pp. xi–xii.
7. Thomas S Kuhn, *The Structure of Scientific Revolutions* (Chicago: University of Chicago, 1962), p. 79.
8. Michael Crichton, *Jurassic Park* (New York: Ballantine Books, 1990), pp. 158, 313.
9. ———., p. 75.
10. Paul Davies, *The Cosmic Blueprint: New Discoveries in Nature's Creative Ability to Order the Universe* (New York: Simon & Schuster), p. 51.
11. ———., p. 53.
12. ———., p. 54.
13. ———., p. 54.
14. Gleick, *Chaos*, pp. 28–29.

15. ———., p. 5.
16. Ivars Peterson and Carol Ezzell, "Crazy Rhythms: Confronting the Complexity of Chaos and Biological Systems," *Science News*, vol. 142, September 5, 1992, pp. 156–59.
17. Stacey, *Managing the Unknowable*, p. 83.

Chapter Two

1. Harry Woodward, *The Change Readiness Survey* (Atlanta, GA: International Learning Inc. and Minneapolis, MN: Woodward Learning International, 1993).
2. Susan J Ashford, "Individual Strategies for Coping with Stress During Organizational Transitions," *The Journal for Applied Behavioral Science*, vol. 24, no. 1, 1988, pp. 19–36.

Chapter Three

1. For background in this area, see the works of Albert Ellis, M C Maultsby, Jr.,; also see E J Garcia and B T Blythe, *Developing Emotional Muscle* (Athens, GA: University of Georgia, 1977).

Chapter Four

1. Ashford, *Individual Strategies*, pp. 30–33.
2. See David Keirsey and Marilyn Bates, *Please Understand Me: Character and Temperament Types* (Del Mar, CA: Prometheus Nemesis Book Company, 1978).

Chapter Five

1. Ashford, *Individual Strategies*, p. 31.
2. Adapted from *Managing Organizational Change*, (Atlanta, GA: ODR, Inc.)
3. Daryl Conner. *Managing at the Speed of Change* (New York: Random House, 1992), pp. 53–4.
4. Quoted by Craig M. Hoffman in *Working Woman Weekends* (*Reader's Digest*, vol. 134, June 1989), pp. 154–60.
5. Harry Woodward and Steve Buchholz, *Aftershock: Helping People through Corporate Change* (New York: John Wiley & Sons, 1987).
6. Ashford, *Individual Strategies*, p. 31.

Chapter Six

1. D H Lawrence, *Studies in Classic American Literature* (New York: The Viking Press, 1961), p. 1.
2. Michael Beer; Russell A Eisenstat; and Bert Spector, "Why Change Programs Don't Produce Change," *Harvard Business Review,* November–December, 1990, p. 159.
3. ———., p. 159.
4. Northrop Frye, *The Great Code: The Bible and Literature* (New York: Harcourt Brace Jovanovich, 1982), p. xv.

Chapter Seven

1. Stanley M Davis, *Future Perfect* (Reading, MA: Addison-Wesley, 1987), p. 24.
2. ———., pp. 24, 27.
3. ———., p. 24.
4. ———., p. 28.
5. See Karl Albrecht, *Brain Power: Learn to Improve Your Thinking Skills* (New York: Prentice Hall, 1980), chap. 4.
6. Davis, *Future Perfect*, p. 28.
7. Ellen J Langer, *Mindfulness* (Reading, MA: Addison-Wesley, 1989), p. 143.
8. Stacey, *Managing the Unknowable*, p. 14.
9. For a detailed discussion of membership, subgrouping, and confrontation, see David L Bradford and Allen R Cohen, *Managing for Excellence* (New York: John Wiley & Sons, 1984).
10. ———., chap. 2.

Bibliography

Alnsworth-Land, George A. *Grow or Die*. New York: John Wiley and Sons. 1986.

Albrecht, Karl. *Brain Power*. New York: Prentice Hall, 1980.

Ashford, Susan J. "Individual Strategies for Coping with Stress During Organizational Transitions." *The Journal for Applied Behavioral Science*. Volume 24, Number 1, 1988, 19–36.

Beer, Michael, et al. "Why Change Programs Don't Produce Change." *Harvard Business Review*. November–December, 1990 p. 150–166.

Belasco, James and Ralph Stayer. *Flight of the Buffalo*. New York: Warner Books, Inc., 1993.

Block, Peter. *The Empowered Manager*. San Francisco, Jossey-Bass, 1991.

Bloom, Allen. *The Closing of the American Mind*. New York: Simon and Schuster, 1987.

Bradford, David L and Allen R Cohen. *Managing for Excellence*. New York: John Wiley and Sons, 1984.

Bridges, William. *Managing Transitions*. Reading, Massachusetts: Addison-Wesley, 1991.

———. *Transitions*. Reading, Massachusetts: Addison-Wesley, 1980.

Conner, Daryl. *Managing at the Speed of Change*. New York: Random House, 1993.

Crichton, Michael. *Jurassic Park*. New York: Random House, 1990.

Davies, Paul. *The Cosmic Blueprint*. New York: Simon and Schuster, 1988.

Davis, Stanley M. *Future Perfect*. Reading, Massachusetts: Addison-Wesley, 1987.

De Bono, Edward. *Six Thinking Hats*. Boston: Little, Brown and Co., 1985.

Drucker, Peter F. *Managing for the Future*. New York: Penguin Books USA Inc., 1992.

———. *Post-Capitalist Society*. New York: Harper Business, 1993.

Ellis, Albert. *How to Stubbornly Refuse to Make Yourself Miserable About Anything!* New York: Lyle Stuart, 1990.

Enright, John. "Change and Resilience." *The Leader Manager.* Eden Prairie, MN: Wilson Learning Corporation, 1985, pp. 59–73.

Frye, Northrop. *The Great Code.* New York: Harcourt Brace Jovanovich, Publishers, 1982.

Gleick, James. *Chaos.* New York: Penguin Books, 1987.

Gray, John. *Men Are from Mars, Women Are from Venus.* New York: HarperCollins, 1992.

Handy, Charles. *The Age of Unreason.* Boston: Harvard Business School Press, 1987.

Henry, Jules. *Culture Against Man.* New York: Random House, 1963.

"Jack Welch's Lessons for Success." *Fortune.* January 25, 1993, pp.86–90.

Jung, Carl G. *Man and His Symbols.* New York: Bantam, 1968.

Kanter, Rosabeth Moss. *The Change Masters.* New York: Simon and Schuster, 1983.

Kroeger, Otto and Janet M. Thuesen. *Type Talk.* New York: Bantam Doubleday Dell, 1988.

Kuhn, Thomas S. *The Structure of Scientific Revolutions.* Chicago: University of Chicago, 1962.

Land, George and Beth Jarman. *Breakpoint and Beyond.* New York: Harper Business, 1992.

Langer, Ellen J. *Mindfulness.* Reading, Massachusetts: Addison-Wesley, 1989.

Lawrence, D H. *Studies in Classic American Literature.* New York: The Viking Press, 1923.

May, Rollo. *The Courage to Create.* New York: Bantam Books, 1976.

Osburn, Jack D, et al. *Self Directed Work Teams.* Homewood, IL: Business One Irwin, 1990.

Pearson, Carol S. *The Hero Within.* San Francisco: Harper Collins, 1986.

Peter, Tom. *Thriving on Chaos.* New York: Alfred A. Knopf, 1987.

Peterson, Ivers and Carol Ezzell. "Crazy Rhythms." *Science News.* Volume 142, September 5, 1992, pp. 156–159.

Polanyi, Michael. *Personal Knowledge.* Chicago: University of Chicago Press, 1962.

Schaffer, Robert H and Harvey A. Thomson. "Successful Change Program Begin with Results," *Harvard Business Review.* January–February 1992, pp. 80–89.

Schumacher, E F A. *A Guide for the Perplexed.* New York: Harper Colophon Books, 1977.

Seligman, Martin E P. *Learned Optimism*. New York: Simon and Schuster, 1990.

Stacey, Ralph D. *Managing the Unknowable*. San Francisco: Jossey-Bass, 1992.

Sternberg, Robert J. *Beyond I. Q.* New York: Cambridge University Press, 1985.

———. *The Triarchic Mind*. New York: Viking, 1988.

Tichy, Noel M. *Managing Strategic Change*. New York: John Wiley & Sons, 1983.

Tichy, Noel and David O. Ulrich. "SMR Forum: The Leadership Challenge—A Call for the Transformational Leader." *Sloan Management Review*. Fall 1984, pp. 59–68.

Toffler, Alvin. *The Adaptive Corporation*. New York: McGraw Hill, 1985.

———. *Future Shock*. New York: Bantam, 1970.

———. *Power Shift*. New York: Bantam, 1990.

———. *The Third Wave*. New York: Bantam, 1980.

Wheatley, Margaret J. *Leadership and the New Science*. San Francisco: Barrett-Koehler, 1992.

Wiebe, Robert H. *The Search for Order 1877–1920*. New York: Hill and Wang, 1967.

Woodward, Harry. "Corporate Renewal or Dreams of Wakefulness." *O. D. Practitioner*. Volume 21, Number 3, September, 1989, pp. 1–5.

———. "Humor Is a Funny Thing." *Resources for Creative Living*, October, 1983, pp. 4–5.

Woodward, Harry and Steve Bachholz. *Aftershock*. New York: John Wiley and Sons, 1987.

Index

Other books of interest to you

THE CHANGE MANAGEMENT HANDBOOK
A Road Map to Corporate Transformation

Lance A. Berger and Martin J. Sikora, with Dorothy R. Berger

With organizations and workers facing inevitable change, today's manager needs the type of concrete, practical guidance this resource provides. Readers will find solutions for managing every stage of the change process—so they can view change as an opportunity, not a crisis. (400 pages)
ISBN: 1-55623-975-0

MANAGING GLOBALLY
A Complete Guide to Competing Worldwide

Carl A. Nelson

With this clear, concise reference, managers will have the step-by-step guidance needed to plan and implement a competitive global strategy. Includes practical checklists, flow charts, and much more. (400 pages)
ISBN: 0-7863-0121-X

MANAGING DIVERSITY
A Complete Desk Reference and Planning Guide

Lee Gardenswartz and Anita Rowe

Co-published with Pfeiffer & Company
This manager's handbook is filled with dozens of planning worksheets and activities designed to encourage high performance levels from diverse employees and cross-cultural teams. Includes creative approaches for mentoring, motivating, and training the workforce. (446 pages)
ISBN: 1-55623-639-5

Available at fine bookstores and libraries everywhere.